Becoming the People of the Mountain

Learning to Live the Sermon on the Mount

Aaron McBride

Becoming the People of the Mountain: Learning to Live the Sermon on the Mount

First Printing 2026

ISBN: 979-8-9997020-1-2

Cover design by Aaron McBride using original artwork and AI-assisted illustration tools.

Published in the United States of America

The author utilized AI-assisted editing and formatting tools to help compile, organize, and refine previously written material. All theological content, teaching, and narrative remain the author's original work.

DEDICATION

For Renee and our children—Aric, Alex, Alton, Ariel, and Ashley—my greatest joy and strength.

And for the people of Victory Baptist Church—thank you for climbing the mountain with me, and for allowing God to shape us into the people of His Kingdom.

Introduction

The title of this book, ***Becoming the People of the Mountain,*** was chosen with purpose. Throughout Scripture, mountains are places where God reveals Himself, where His voice is heard, and where His people are changed. When Jesus sat down on a hillside and began to teach what we now call the Sermon on the Mount, He wasn't offering abstract ideals or lofty philosophy. He was inviting ordinary people into not only a new way of life, but into His Kingdom—a Kingdom life and way that reshapes the heart, reorders desires, and redefines what it means to follow Him. To become the people of the Mountain is to take Jesus at His word and allow His word to take hold of us.

For more than two years, our church family walked slowly through these three chapters in Matthew—verse by verse, week by week. What began as a sermon series gradually became something much deeper. There were Sundays I left the pulpit more convicted than encouraged. More than once, I found myself preaching a passage that had already exposed something in my own heart. The Sermon on the Mount stopped being material to teach and became a mirror I could not avoid.

These chapters revealed how easily I can admire Jesus without fully obeying Him. They exposed how often I settle for outward compliance while neglecting inward surrender. And yet, they also reminded me that the Kingdom life Jesus describes is not burdensome—it is beautiful. It is demanding, yes. But it is also freeing.

As I studied and taught through these passages, I found myself confronted again and again by the radical simplicity of Jesus' call. The Sermon on the Mount does not merely inform the mind; it reforms the life. It does not ask for admiration; it calls for transformation. These words are not distant ideals—they are invitations. Invitations to live differently, to love differently, to trust differently. Invitations to become the kind of people who reflect the heart of the King—a people marked by mercy, purity, forgiveness, humility, courage, and Kingdom hope.

When Jesus sat down on that hillside and opened His mouth to teach, He was calling ordinary people into a way of life unlike anything they had ever known. Not a life defined by outward religion, but a life shaped by inward transformation—a life shaped by humility and mercy, strengthened by courage, grounded in purity, and overflowing with forgiveness and Kingdom hope. A life that reflects the heart of God to the world.

This book is not meant to be a commentary or an academic exploration, though you will certainly find careful study within its pages. It is not meant to be a theological textbook, though it is grounded in the rich truth of Scripture. Instead, this book is an invitation—an invitation to join the journey of becoming. Becoming more like Jesus. Becoming more aligned with His Kingdom. Becoming people who live the blessed, beautiful, counter-cultural life Jesus describes on the mountain. ***Becoming the people of the Mountain***.

My prayer is that as you read these chapters, you will hear the voice of Jesus calling you upward. That you will sense His nearness, His authority, and His love. That the teachings of the Sermon on the Mount will not merely inform your understanding, but transform your way of living. And that, together, we will become what He intended us to be all along: *the people of the Mountain, shaped by the words of the King*.

Welcome to the climb. May He meet you on every step of it.

CONTENTS

Chapter 1
The Character of the Kingdom: The Beatitudes

Matthew 5:1–12

1 Now seeing the crowds, He went up on a mountain. And when He sat down, His disciples came to Him.

2 And He began speaking and taught them, saying:

3 "Blessed are the poor in spirit, for theirs is the kingdom of heaven.

4 Blessed are those who mourn, for they shall be comforted.

5 Blessed are the meek, for they shall inherit the earth.

6 Blessed are those who hunger and thirst for righteousness, for they shall be filled.

7 Blessed are the merciful, for they shall obtain mercy.

8 Blessed are the pure in heart, for they shall see God.

9 Blessed are the peacemakers, for they shall be called the sons of God.

10 Blessed are those who are persecuted for righteousness' sake, for theirs is the kingdom of heaven.

11 "Blessed are you when men revile you, and persecute you, and say all kinds of evil against you falsely for My sake.

12 Rejoice and be very glad, because great is your reward in heaven, for in this manner they persecuted the prophets who were before you.

Pastor's Reflection

Before Jesus ever spoke the first word of the Sermon on the Mount, Matthew tells us something essential—something that shaped how I approached this entire two-year journey with our church.

Matthew 4 paints the picture: Jesus is moving through Galilee, preaching the good news of the Kingdom, healing every disease, touching broken bodies and broken spirits. Crowds from every direction begin pressing in—Galilee, the Decapolis, Jerusalem, Judea, and beyond the Jordan. They come limping, crawling, desperate, hungry. They bring their sick, their demon-oppressed, their paralyzed.

They bring their stories, their pain, their longing—and Jesus meets them there, healing them one by one.

It is only after all of this—after compassion, after restoration, after calling fishermen to follow Him—that Jesus goes up the mountain.

The Sermon on the Mount is not given to the proud or the curious, but to the desperate who followed Him up the hill. To those who had already tasted His mercy and wanted more. To those who had left nets, routines, and reputations behind because something in His voice awakened a hunger for which they didn't have words.

When I look back at the beginning of this journey for our church, I see something similar.

We didn't begin this study from a season of strength; we began from a place of need. We were coming through seasons of transition, wounds, unanswered questions, and deep longing for God to steady us and shape us. Just like the crowds in Matthew 4, we were hungry for what only Jesus could do.

And Jesus, in His kindness, brought us to the mountain.

We didn't know it then, but the Beatitudes would become a mirror held up to our hearts and a window into the kind of people Jesus was forming us to be.

The kind of people we are always shapes how we live.

Before Jesus tells us how to live, He addresses who we are becoming. The heart comes first. The rest flows from there.

Matthew 4 taught me something I held close through every week of this study: Jesus brings people to the mountain after He has first shown them His mercy.

We do not climb the mountain to earn a place in the Kingdom. We come because the King has already drawn near and invited us up.

This is where the journey begins—not with our worthiness, but with His invitation.

The Beatitudes: The Portrait of Kingdom People

Jesus does not begin the Sermon on the Mount with a list of rules. He begins by describing a kind of person.

Before He speaks about anger or lust or prayer or enemies, He talks about the heart. He shows us what life looks like when God is doing something deep inside someone.

When we first began walking through these verses as a church, I assumed we were starting a study. Over time, I realized something else was happening. The Beatitudes were not just explaining the Kingdom to us—they were quietly exposing us.

They did not feel impressive. They felt honest.

At first, they sound upside down. The people Jesus calls blessed are not the strong, the admired, or the visibly successful. They are the ones who know their need. The ones who grieve. The ones who do not push themselves forward.

It forces you to slow down and ask, "Is this really what a flourishing life looks like?"

As we sat with these words week after week, I began to see that the Beatitudes are less about collecting virtues and more about recognizing transformation. They describe what begins to grow in someone who has come close to Jesus and stayed there.

You start to see patterns.

Poverty of spirit humbles you.

Mourning softens you.

Meekness steadies you.

Hunger for righteousness reorients your desires.

Mercy reshapes the way you treat people.

Purity simplifies your motives.

Peacemaking sends you toward conflict instead of away from it.

And persecution reveals who you truly belong to.

None of these qualities can be forced. They are not personality traits. They are not spiritual achievements. They grow slowly in a life that keeps turning back to Christ.

That is why Jesus begins here.

Long before He speaks about the narrow road or secret prayer or loving enemies, He shows us the kind of heart that can live that way.

The Beatitudes are not requirements to get into the Kingdom. They are signs that the Kingdom has begun to take root in you.

This is what the mountain is shaping in us.

This is where becoming begins.

What Does "Blessed" Really Mean?

Before we walk through each Beatitude, we need to slow down here. If we misunderstand this single word – blessed – we will misunderstand everything Jesus is about to say.

In English, the word can sound soft or sentimental. We say, "I'm blessed," when life feels good, when things are going our way, or when we are comfortable. But that is not what Jesus means.

The Greek word *makarios* was familiar to His original hearers. It carries the idea of being favored by God, fortunate in His sight, even privileged in a way that has nothing to do with status or wealth. Some translate it as happy, but not in the shallow sense of passing emotion. It points to a deeper well-being.

It describes a life that is approved by God. A life that rests in Him. A kind of settled wholeness that circumstances cannot finally undo.

Blessed does not describe how life looks on the outside; it speaks to how God sees a person who belongs to His Kingdom.

That means someone can be grieving and still be blessed.

They can be struggling, under pressure, or misunderstood – and still be favored in the eyes of God.

Blessedness is not rooted in our situation but in our standing with the King.

During this series, I watched many in our church wrestle with that truth. Some realized for the first time that Jesus was not calling them to chase happiness. He was inviting them into a life anchored in God's approval rather than public applause.

This is why the Beatitudes sound so different from the world's definition of a good life. Jesus is not pointing to people who appear fortunate. He is declaring that those who depend on Him are the ones who are truly secure.

Blessedness, in the end, is God's declaration over those who come to Him empty and honest.

It is His way of saying, "These are My people."

Poor in Spirit

As our church began this journey, it didn't take long for me to realize why Jesus starts here. Week after week, I watched God gently peel back layers of self-reliance in sincere believers—men and women who, like me, often carried the quiet assumption that we could handle life on our own.

To be *poor in spirit* is where we begin—with the honest confession that we have nothing. Jesus places this Beatitude first because nothing else in the Christian life can be built on pride. Spiritual poverty does not mean despising ourselves. It means being honest before God about our need and coming to Him without pretending we have it together. It is stepping into the presence of God with empty hands and a dependent heart.

There were Sundays when the room felt especially still—as if the Spirit Himself was reminding us that the Kingdom of God does not rise on how capable or put-together we think we are. It rises in hearts that know their need.

In a world obsessed with self-confidence, Jesus blesses those who know they are spiritually bankrupt. This is the Kingdom's first shock: blessedness begins with brokenness. The doorway into life with God is low enough that only the humble can enter.

Spiritual poverty may look like weakness from the outside, but in truth it brings a kind of clarity. It helps us see ourselves rightly before God and loosens our grip on the need to prove anything. It is the moment we stop performing for God and start depending on Him. Being poor in spirit is less about trying harder and more about finally letting go. It is learning, sometimes slowly and sometimes painfully, to trust God with what we cannot fix in ourselves.

Those Who Mourn

I remember realizing early on that this Beatitude wasn't calling us to walk around solemn or heavy—it was calling us into a deeper honesty than most of us were used to. As people shared their stories, confessed burdens, and opened their hearts, I saw a kind of freedom begin to emerge in our church. Grief, when brought to Jesus, was not crushing. It was cleansing.

If poverty of spirit is seeing our condition, mourning is feeling it. Jesus blesses those who grieve their sin, because grief is the birthplace of repentance. This is not the mourning of despair, but of awakening—the kind of mourning that drives us toward the mercy of God rather than away from Him.

True mourning is not simply sorrow over consequences but sorrow over the condition of our hearts. It is the Spirit-produced ache that says, "I cannot stay this way." And to such mourning, Jesus attaches a promise: *they shall be comforted.*

But this mourning is not only personal—it is also missional. As we walked through this Beatitude, many in our church began to feel a deeper grief over the brokenness of the world around us. The same Spirit who convicts us of our own sin also softens our hearts toward those who are still far from Christ. Kingdom people don't just mourn the darkness within; they mourn the darkness without. They feel the ache of a world that does not know its Savior, and that grief becomes fuel for compassion, prayer, and gospel courage.

I cannot count how many times during this series I watched people wiped clean by that comfort. Not condemned. Not shamed. Comforted. The comfort He gives is not merely emotional relief—it is the deep, soul-settling assurance of forgiveness and restoration.

This Beatitude reminds us that the Christian life is marked not by perfection, but by repentance. The holiest people are not those who never fail, but those who continually return to the Father who welcomes prodigals home.

The Meek

Meekness tested us—individually and as a church. There

were seasons when tensions rose, opinions clashed, and people wrestled with change. And yet, I watched something beautiful happen: instead of doubling down, many leaned back into trust. Meekness began to reshape our relationships.

Meekness includes humility, because at its core it is about placing our strength under God's authority. Humility requires us to take whatever strength we have—our voice, our convictions, our abilities—and place them under God's authority. Meekness can look like weakness from the outside, but what is really happening is that a person has chosen to place their strength under God's direction rather than using it to push their own way forward.

The meek are those who have laid down the weapons of self-assertion and entrusted themselves and their future to the Father. They are not passive. They are submitted.

In a culture that celebrates dominance, Jesus blesses those who live differently—those who do not demand center stage, those who do not retaliate in anger, those who trust God to defend them. Meekness frees us from the exhausting need to control outcomes or win every argument.

I saw meekness in parents navigating hard seasons, in friends working through strained relationships, in believers choosing gentleness when conflict offered them an easier route. The meek may not look impressive in the eyes of the world, but heaven sees something steady and strong.

Jesus attaches a promise to this kind of life: *they shall inherit the earth.* It is something received from God rather than something we try to seize or negotiate for ourselves. The meek trust God enough to wait for what He gives rather than grasp for what they think they deserve.

Those Who Hunger and Thirst for Righteousness

I could feel this one in the room—hunger.

People were asking deeper questions and spending more time searching the Scriptures.

Many people were beginning to realize that small spiritual adjustments were not enough. Something deeper needed to change.

We wanted transformation.

As we talked through this together, it became clear how much of life is shaped by what we long for. Jesus redirects that hunger toward the only source that satisfies—righteousness. This is not the hunger for self-improvement or moral polish, but a deep longing for the life of God to reshape us from the inside out.

That kind of hunger begins to align our desires with what God desires. It is a longing that refuses spiritual apathy. And Jesus promises that such hunger will be met: they shall be filled.

I remember thinking how often we settle for spiritual snacks—moments of inspiration—when Jesus is inviting us to a feast. The Spirit does not ignore those who seek holiness—He satisfies them, strengthens them, and changes them.

Righteousness does not come from our effort or our ability to improve ourselves. It is something God gives to those who come to Him hungry for it and willing to depend on Christ. But it is received only by those who hunger for it.

This Beatitude gives us the freedom to admit our need and the confidence that Christ supplies what we lack.

The Merciful

This Beatitude became real in the small, often unseen moments of our church life—conversations where patience was needed and reconciliations that took courage. Sometimes forgiveness came slowly, but mercy began quietly shaping our culture. Mercy began quietly shaping our culture.

Mercy is what happens when grace transforms the way we see others. Those who have tasted the kindness of God cannot withhold kindness from their neighbors. Mercy moves us toward people the world avoids. It leads us to forgive offenses the world prefers to keep remembering, and it teaches us to show compassion even when others see that as weakness.

The merciful understand that God has not dealt with them according to their sins—and so they refuse to deal harshly with others. Mercy is not ignoring sin; it is responding to people with the same patience and tenderness that Jesus has shown to us.

I saw mercy begin to change people, and I watched it take root in the life of a dear woman in our church. Her daughter and son-in-law had taken advantage of her and treated her with deep disregard, offering no apology and showing no remorse. Yet she continued to extend mercy—real, costly mercy—choosing forgiveness over bitterness, compassion over resentment. Her quiet faithfulness became a simple example of what this Beatitude looks like in real life. And Jesus gives this promise: *they shall obtain mercy.*

The merciful live with the ongoing awareness that God is gentle with them. When someone begins to grasp how patient and merciful God has been with them, it slowly begins to change the way they treat other people. The mercy they have received starts to show up in the mercy they extend.

The Pure in Heart

As we studied this Beatitude, I began hearing people talk about wanting God to clear away the things that kept crowding their hearts and pulling their attention in different directions. Purity of heart often grows quietly. You do not always notice it at first, but over time its effects become clear in the way a person lives.

Purity of heart does not mean a person never struggles with sin. It speaks of a heart that is being drawn toward a single devotion to God rather than being pulled in many different directions. The pure heart is the heart that wants one thing—God. In a world of endless distractions, Jesus blesses those whose inner life is not fragmented by competing loves.

In many ways it begins with simple integrity, learning to be the same person in private that we appear to be in public. It grows as we practice confession and stay rooted in Scripture. Over time, that kind of life deepens through communion with Christ. Those who are pure in heart are not perfect, but they are honest.

During these weeks, I heard people talk about simplifying their lives, cutting out spiritual noise, and removing distractions that dulled their devotion. Purity clears the lens — and for many in our church, it was like God wiped the fog from a window we hadn't realized was clouded.

And Jesus promises something remarkable: *they shall see God.* Not just someday in heaven, but now—in worship, in His Word, in answered prayer, in the quiet moments when His presence becomes unmistakably real.

The Peacemakers

This was perhaps one of the most stretching seasons for us as a church. Peacemaking pushed us to listen more carefully and slow down before responding. It also meant learning to pursue restoration rather than simply trying to win the moment. I watched believers take brave steps toward one another—steps that required humility and the Spirit's help.

Peacemakers do not merely love peace—they *make* it. They step into conflict with the heart of Christ, seeking restoration rather than victory. Their ministry begins with the gospel: first helping people find peace with God, and then helping them walk in peace with one another.

Peacemaking takes humility and patience, and it usually begins with learning to listen well. It rejects the shortcuts of blame or avoidance. It seeks the good of the other person, even when doing so is costly.

I saw peacemaking in hallway conversations and in late-night phone calls. I also saw it in forgiveness offered after months of hurt. These small acts—all unseen by the world—were deeply seen by God.

Jesus calls them something remarkable: *they shall be called the children of God.* Why? Because peacemakers resemble their Father. The God who reconciled us to Himself through Christ now forms His people into instruments of reconciliation. When we step toward peace, we step into the family likeness.

Every act of peace—whether it restores a relationship, quiets a conflict, or brings clarity where there was confusion—whispers the truth of the gospel to a watching world.

The Persecuted

The final Beatitude brings a kind of clarity that the others slowly prepare us for. Jesus makes it clear that following Him will attract opposition—not because His people are abrasive or arrogant, but because righteousness exposes darkness.

The kind of persecution Jesus is describing is not about being harsh, foolish, or argumentative. It is the cost of living a life shaped by the Kingdom. When we walk in purity, humility, mercy, and truth, some will be drawn to Christ—but others will resist.

And yet Jesus still calls the persecuted *blessed*. Why? Because their suffering is evidence of their identity: *theirs is the Kingdom of Heaven.* Their loyalty to Christ marks them as citizens of another world. And Jesus attaches another promise—*great is your reward in heaven.*

Moments like this have a way of revealing where our allegiance truly lies. In seasons when following Christ costs something, we begin to see more clearly what we actually trust and who we are living for. It teaches us to live for eternity and reminds us that the applause of God outweighs the rejection of man.

Reflection & Practice

The Beatitudes present us with a question far deeper than "How am I doing?" They invite us to ask, "Who am I becoming?" These eight statements form the groundwork for everything Jesus teaches in the chapters that follow. They are not a checklist but a calling—a description of the life the Spirit produces in those who walk with Jesus.

As I watched our church walk this out, I began asking myself questions like these — and now I offer them to you:

- Which Beatitude is Christ cultivating most clearly in you right now?
- Which one do you resist the most—and why?
- How might Jesus be inviting you to surrender your strength, your plans, or your expectations to become more like Him?

The journey up the mountain begins here—not with our efforts, but with His transforming grace. As we walk through the Sermon on the Mount, these Beatitudes will remain our compass, reminding us who Jesus is shaping us to be.

Chapter 2
The People of Influence: Salt and Light

Matthew 5:13–16

13 You are the salt of the earth. But if the salt loses its saltiness, how shall it be made salty? It is from then on good for nothing but to be thrown out and to be trampled underfoot by men.

14 You are the light of the world. A city that is set on a hill cannot be hidden.

15 Neither do men light a candle and put it under a basket, but on a candlestick. And it gives light to all who are in the house.
16 Let your light so shine before men that they may see your good works and glorify your Father who is in heaven.

Pastor's Reflection

Before we ever reached Jesus' words about salt and light, the Lord had already begun doing something in our church. For me, that part of the story started quietly in June of 2024. I was praying about the preaching calendar and asking the Lord where we should go next. Again and again my thoughts kept returning to the Sermon on the Mount. I didn't fully understand why at the time. I only knew the sense that we were supposed to slow down and walk through those words together.

When I began laying out the calendar, I noticed something I hadn't planned. Matthew 5:13–16—"You are the salt of the earth… you are the light of the world"—was scheduled right after the dates of May 4–6, 2025. I hadn't arranged that intentionally. Only later did I realize how meaningful that timing would become.

In early May of 2025 our city experienced something we had been praying for. During the Night of Hope event in Fallon, many people came to Christ. Families began reconnecting with the Lord, and conversations about faith started happening across our community. It was one of those moments that reminds you God is still working in ways we could never plan ourselves.

And then, right after those days, we arrived at Matthew 5:13–16.

Standing there with those words in front of us—"You are the salt of the earth… you are the light of the world"—our church stepped into the "Who's Your One" challenge. It wasn't something we had planned months earlier. The passage itself stirred it. We simply asked everyone in our church to begin praying for one person they could pursue with the gospel over the next year.

Names weren't written down until that moment. But once they were, something changed in our church. People began praying intentionally for neighbors, coworkers, friends, and family members who were far from Christ. Some of those names were spoken through tears, while others were simply carried quietly in prayer week after week.

Over time we began hearing the stories. God was opening doors. Conversations were happening. Some of those people began coming to church. And some of them, by God's grace, came to faith in Christ.

There was also a growing awareness among us that God had placed us in Fallon for a reason. People showed up on Sundays carrying the names of the people they were praying for—a son who had drifted from the Lord or a coworker asking hard questions about faith.

So when Launch Sunday arrived—the Sunday we paused the Sermon on the Mount to focus directly on mission—it didn't feel like a separate idea. It felt like the next step in what God had already begun among us.

Families prayed together before the service, and new believers walked in with a kind of expectancy. Longtime members looked around the room with a quiet sense that God was writing a story that was bigger than any of us.

Launch Sunday wasn't simply the start of a program. It felt more like a marker in the life of our church—a moment when we realized that God had been preparing us long before we understood what He was doing.

And when we returned to Matthew 5 the following week, the words of Jesus sounded different to us. They weren't theoretical anymore. They were personal.

Because before Jesus sends His people into the world, He forms

[1]Who's Your One?' is a resource and initiative originally developed by the North American Mission Board. We adapted the heart of that idea in our local context.

something inside them. After shaping His disciples through the Beatitudes, He turns to them and begins to talk about their influence.

In other words, once He shows them who they are becoming, He begins to show them why it matters.

The Calling That Flows From Character

Jesus doesn't begin the Sermon on the Mount by talking about mission. He starts by forming a people. Only after shaping their hearts through the Beatitudes does He speak about their influence. In other words:

Identity comes before assignment.

You cannot be salt and light if the Beatitudes are not taking root in your life. Jesus is not giving His disciples a list of ideals to chase after. He is describing the kind of people they are becoming as they follow Him.

The world isn't changed by impressive people. What it needs are people whose lives are being changed by Christ.

When humility, repentance, and mercy begin to take hold, something shifts in a person. Others start to notice it—not because the believer is trying to stand out, but because the life of Christ is beginning to show through ordinary choices and everyday faithfulness.

That kind of influence rarely looks dramatic. It rarely grows out of platform or visibility. Instead, it grows quietly through a life that keeps walking with Jesus.

You Are the Salt of the Earth

In the ancient world, salt was precious. It preserved what was good, purified what was unclean, and enhanced what was bland. Jesus intentionally chose something common yet invaluable to describe His people.

1. Salt Preserves

The world is not morally neutral. It slowly drifts and corrodes over time. And Jesus sends His people into the world as a preserving presence—holding back decay through righteousness and truth.

You may not always notice this influence, but it's there: in the quiet decisions you make, the integrity you maintain and the patience you show.

2. Salt Purifies

Salt was rubbed into meat to prevent corruption. In the same way, the presence of God's people pushes against the corruption of sin—not with anger or arrogance, but with holiness and conviction.

A believer who walks in purity makes it harder for sin to feel comfortable.

3. Salt Enhances Flavor

Salt brings out what is hidden, and even a small amount can change the whole flavor. Jesus is saying that kingdom people make the world taste different. We bring hope into hurting lives and grace into bitter spaces.

Wherever God has placed you—your home, workplace, school, or neighborhood—He intends you to bring out the goodness He planted there.

The Warning: Losing Saltiness

Jesus' warning is sobering: "If the salt loses its saltiness..." In His day, salt was often blended with other minerals. It might look like salt, pour like salt, and be stored like salt—but without its true essence, it could no longer do what it was meant to do.

This is a picture of a disciple who keeps the appearance of Christianity but loses the substance of it.

Losing saltiness doesn't usually happen suddenly. It happens slowly, often when compromise becomes normal—when small concessions turn into familiar patterns. As conviction grows quiet and the voice of the Spirit becomes easier to ignore. It happens when the Beatitudes no longer shape our character but become distant words on a page. and sometimes when we blend in so comfortably with the culture that no one notices a difference anymore.

This kind of quiet drift doesn't change our vocabulary, but it changes our impact.

Jesus is warning against a diluted discipleship—a faith that still carries Christian vocabulary but no longer carries Kingdom power.

Salt can only influence if it is different.

And He doesn't soften the warning: a life that loses its distinctiveness loses its impact. The world doesn't need a church that echoes its own values back to it. It needs a people whose lives carry a different flavor—truth with grace and purity with compassion.

The good news is that saltiness is not something we produce—it's something we protect. We stay salty by staying close to Jesus and remaining tender to the conviction of His Spirit as He forms His character in us through the Beatitudes.

You Are the Light of the World

Salt describes the quiet influence of a life shaped by Jesus—its hidden strength, its preserving presence, its steady, faithful impact. But Jesus doesn't stop with what His followers are beneath the surface. He moves to what they are in full view of the world.

Salt tends to work quietly and almost unnoticed, but light is different—it shows up in a way that people can see. Light cuts through darkness and draws attention, creating contrast. And with this shift in imagery, Jesus widens the lens. He moves from the disciple's private integrity to their public witness.

He is saying, in effect:

"The work I am doing in you is not meant to stay in you."

Your faith isn't meant to remain a hidden ingredient. Over time it becomes something people can see in the way you live. Grace is not something God plants only in the quiet soil of the heart; over time it grows into something people can see and begin to follow.

With that in mind, Jesus makes a staggering statement:

"You are the light of the world."

Not the elite. Not the religious experts. Not the influencers or the powerful. Ordinary disciples. And He gives them the same title He gave Himself.

1. Light Reveals What Is True

Light exposes what is hidden—not to shame, but to heal. Your life, shaped by the Beatitudes, reveals the truth about God to people who are searching, hurting, or wandering.

Many people will first encounter Jesus not through a sermon, but through your life.

2. Light Guides Others Home

A city on a hill was a beacon of safety for travelers. The Christian life is meant to be lived visibly—not arrogantly, but authentically. When people watch you walk with Jesus, they should see a path that leads them toward Him.

Your faith becomes a signpost.

3. Light Draws People to God, Not to You

Jesus is clear: *"That they may see your good works and glorify your Father who is in heaven."* The goal of shining is not attention—it is direction. Your life should not point to your goodness but to God's grace.

The good works Jesus speaks of are the visible obedience that grows out of the Beatitudes. When humility, mercy, and purity begin to shape your life, those works become a light that directs hearts toward the Father.

The Temptation: Hiding the Light

Jesus says no one lights a lamp only to hide it. Yet we often do—sometimes without even realizing it. If the warning about salt speaks to *losing what makes us distinct*, the warning about light speaks to *refusing to display what God has already placed within us.*

Fear can keep us silent when our voice is needed. Insecurity may convince us that we have nothing meaningful to offer, and shame can whisper that our past disqualifies us from shining at all. At other times comfort makes blending in feel easier than standing out, and the desire for approval causes us to dim the truth we were called to display.

All of these become the quiet ways a lamp gets covered—still burning, but unable to help anyone see.

But Jesus insists that light was made for visibility—not for spotlight, but for service. A lamp wasn't placed there simply to be admired; its purpose was to help people see their way.

A hidden lamp is as useless as flavorless salt. Both lose their purpose when they cease to function as intended.

And here is the grace: Jesus isn't scolding His disciples—He is reminding them of who they are. Light doesn't strain to shine; it simply shines because of what it is. The more His character takes shape within us, the more naturally His light shines through us.

The Mission Jesus Gives His People

Salt and light are not tasks Jesus assigns; they describe who His people already are. Jesus does not say, "Try to be salt and light." He says, *"You are salt. You are light."*

When Jesus says His people are salt and light, He is declaring that influence is part of what it means to follow Christ, and the work of His kingdom isn't limited to a few especially gifted people or a select group with a special calling. Every disciple plays a part.

God has placed you exactly where you are—your street, your workplace, your school, your friendships, your routines, your conversations—not by randomness but by design.

These places are not accidents; they are assignments.

And when the Beatitudes shape your life, you carry the presence and truth of Jesus into every one of them—and often in ways you may not fully see in the moment, but that God is quietly shaping over time.

Reflection & Practice

Before you move on, pause for a moment. Jesus' words in this passage are not meant to be admired from a distance—they are meant to be lived. Salt and light are identities that show up in the ordinary rhythms of your week, your conversations, your relationships, and your choices. These questions are an invitation to slow down, reflect deeply, and step intentionally into the influence Jesus has already given you.

- Where has God placed you as salt—quietly preserving, purifying, or enhancing the world around you?
- Where is fear or complacency tempting you to hide your light instead of letting it shine?
- Who in your life may need the influence of your presence, words, or compassion this week?
- What small act of obedience could make Christ's light visible in your daily routine?

Let your light shine—not to draw eyes to yourself, but to direct hearts toward the Father.

Chapter 3
The Law Fulfilled: Jesus and the Scriptures

Matthew 5:17–20

17 Do not think that I have come to abolish the Law or the Prophets. I have not come to abolish, but to fulfill.

18 For truly I say to you, until heaven and earth pass away, not one dot or one mark will pass from the law until all be fulfilled.

19 Whoever, therefore, breaks one of the least of these commandments and teaches others to do likewise shall be called the least in the kingdom of heaven. But whoever does and teaches them shall be called great in the kingdom of heaven.

20 For I say to you that unless your righteousness exceeds the righteousness of the scribes and Pharisees, you will in no way enter the kingdom of heaven.

Pastor's Reflection

Before Jesus spoke a single word about anger, lust, and even enemy love, He paused to clear the air about something His listeners would have assumed: that His teaching contradicted the Scriptures they revered.

This moment has always stood out to me. Long before our church ever reached this passage in our verse-by-verse journey, my own heart wrestled with the tension many believers feel. We look at the Old Testament and sometimes wonder what to do with it. Some avoid it altogether, while others lean on it so heavily that they lose sight of the gospel. And many misunderstand the relationship between the Law and the gospel.

But for me, the clarity began long before our church reached this passage. As I reflected on Jesus' words, I sensed that what He said here about the Law and the Prophets would become I began to realize how central these words were to what Jesus says next.

I didn't know then how necessary it would be.

As we walked through the Beatitudes, our church began to experience a renewed hunger for genuine discipleship, for the kind of character that only Jesus can form in His people. Then came the call to be salt and light—a call we lived out in real time as God moved through Night of Hope and the "Who's Your One" challenge.

But as Jesus shaped our hearts toward mission, He also led us into this passage, where He addressed a question that still affects believers today:

What do we do with the Scriptures Jesus Himself fulfilled?

What I love about this moment is that Jesus doesn't apologize for the Law. He doesn't diminish it. He doesn't distance Himself from it. He honors it. He upholds it. And yet, He does something far deeper—He shows how every line points to Him.

This passage became a turning point for many in our church. It helped people lay down old fears rooted in legalism. It helped others see that grace is not opposed to obedience. And it helped us all understand that the Scriptures are not a burden to escape but a story fulfilled in the One who came to rescue us.

As I prepared this chapter, I revisited those early days of study and the journey we took as a congregation. What stayed with me was this: Jesus was not giving us a new religion. He was giving us Himself—the fulfillment of everything God had promised.

And it changed the way we read the Bible.

The Misunderstood Mission

Jesus begins this section with a clarification: *"Do not think that I have come to abolish the Law or the Prophets."* The very fact that He starts this way tells us something important—people were already assuming the opposite.

His authority, His miracles, His message of grace, His conflicts with religious leaders—all of it led many to wonder whether He was discarding centuries of Scripture. But Jesus wanted His disciples to know exactly why He came.

He did not come to erase the Scriptures but to fulfill them.

The Law and the Prophets were not being replaced. They were reaching their intended destination.

In the same way a seed finds its fulfillment in a tree, or a promise in its completion, the Scriptures find their fulfillment in Jesus.

Everything God had spoken, commanded, foreshadowed, or prepared was leading to Him.

How Jesus Fulfilled the Scriptures

Fulfillment does not mean cancellation; it means something has finally reached the purpose it was always meant to serve.

Jesus fulfilled the Scriptures in several ways:

1. He Fulfilled the Moral Law Through Perfect Obedience

Where every human has failed, Jesus succeeded. He kept the Law not only outwardly but inwardly. His obedience revealed the holiness of God in human form.

2. He Fulfilled the Ceremonial Law by Completing Its Purpose

The sacrifices, rituals, and temple system were all shadows pointing forward. Jesus, the Lamb of God, was the reality those shadows anticipated. He didn't abolish the ceremonial law—He completed it.

3. He Fulfilled the Prophetic Law by Being Its Promised Messiah

Every prophecy about the coming Redeemer found its "Yes and Amen" in Him. The prophets were signposts, and Jesus was the destination.

Everything the Law demanded, He satisfied. Everything the Prophets foretold, He embodied. Jesus didn't discard the Old Testament—He revealed its fullness.

The Permanence of Scripture

Jesus continues by saying, *"Until heaven and earth pass away, not one jot or one tittle shall pass from the Law until all is fulfilled."* In a world where many dismiss Scripture as outdated, irrelevant, or the product of ancient minds detached from modern life, Jesus speaks with unmistakable authority.

He is not lowering the value of the Old Testament. He is raising it beyond every cultural critique.

People today call the Scriptures primitive, old-fashioned, or the writings of "goat herders" lacking understanding. But Jesus makes a radically different claim: **the Word of God is more permanent than the world itself.** Heaven and earth will pass away before a single stroke of Scripture becomes void.

Every detail points to something about God's holiness, humanity's need, and the redemption fulfilled in Christ.

This means Scripture isn't fragile—it's indestructible, something that rises above time. It isn't shaped by culture—it confronts and transforms culture.

The Scriptures are not outdated relics. They are not optional. They are not flexible suggestions. They stand firm until God's purposes are fully realized.

Great and Least in the Kingdom

Jesus' next statement may surprise modern readers. He draws a distinction between those who take God's commands lightly—and teach others to do the same—and those who honor God's commands and point others toward obedience.

This is not a ranking system meant to puff up egos. It is a window into what heaven values.

In our world, greatness is measured by influence, visibility, or achievement. But in the kingdom of heaven, greatness is measured by faithfulness. Jesus is revealing that a humble believer who seeks to honor God's Word—quietly, consistently, even imperfectly—is considered *great* in His kingdom.

And the opposite is just as true: someone who dismisses Scripture, minimizes obedience, or leads others to lower their view of God's commands is missing the very heartbeat of the kingdom.

This is not about earning salvation. It is about aligning our lives with the God we claim to love.

What Jesus elevates here is the posture of a teachable heart—a heart that says, *"Lord, Your Word matters. Help me live it and help me lead others toward it."*

Obedience is not legalism when it flows from love. It is the joyful response of a heart transformed by grace.

The Greater Righteousness

Jesus concludes this section with a statement that would have stunned His audience: *"Unless your righteousness exceeds that of the scribes and Pharisees, you will in no case enter the kingdom of heaven."*

To the average listener, this sounded impossible. The scribes and Pharisees were the religious elite—the ones who looked flawless from the outside. Their lives were wrapped in outward obedience, rituals, practices, and tradition. They appeared to be the standard.

But Jesus was not raising the bar of performance. He was shifting the location of righteousness altogether.

The Pharisees focused on **external compliance**—keeping rules, maintaining appearances, managing behavior. Jesus was calling His followers to **internal transformation**—a righteousness that begins in the heart, reshapes desires, and produces authentic obedience.

The point is not doing more than the Pharisees. It is about becoming different from them.

This greater righteousness is not rooted in fear, but in love. It is born through the work of the Spirit rather than produced by human effort. And it does not flow from old habits but from a new heart transformed by grace. The righteousness Jesus describes is not something we achieve through our own strength—it is the very righteousness of Christ credited to us through faith and formed in us through the Spirit.

Over time I began to see that the Sermon on the Mount wasn't meant to function like a checklist. It is a portrait of what life in the kingdom looks like when God transforms a person from the inside out.

And this sets the stage for everything Jesus will say next. Every command that follows—about anger, lust, forgiveness, truthfulness, and love—grows out of this greater righteousness that only He can give. The rest of Matthew 5 is not a list of external requirements—it is an invitation into a life shaped from the inside out by the grace and truth of Jesus.

Reflection & Practice

The words of Jesus in Matthew 5:17–20 invite us to rethink the Scriptures—not as a burden, but as a revelation of the One who fulfilled them.

Consider:

- How does seeing Jesus as the fulfillment of the Scriptures change the way you read the Old Testament?
- Are there areas where you have misunderstood obedience as legalism, or grace as permission to avoid holiness?
- What would it look like for the righteousness of Christ to shape your heart rather than simply guide your behavior?
- How might this passage prepare you for the deeper heart-level teachings Jesus gives next?

Let His words draw you into a deeper love for the Scriptures and the Savior who fulfilled them.

Chapter 4

The Silent Killer: Anger, Bitterness and the Way Back

Matthew 5:21–26

21 You have heard that it was said by the ancients, "You shall not murder," and "Whoever murders shall be in danger of the judgment."

22 But I say to you that whoever is angry with his brother without a cause shall be in danger of the judgment. And whoever says to his brother, "Raca," shall be in danger of the Sanhedrin. But whoever says, "You fool," shall be in danger of hell fire.

23 Therefore, if you bring your gift to the altar and there remember that your brother has something against you,

24 Leave your gift there before the altar and go on your way. First be reconciled to your brother, and then come and offer your gift.

25 Reconcile with your adversary quickly, while you are on the way with him, lest your adversary deliver you to the judge, and the judge deliver you to the officer, and you be thrown into prison.

26 Truly I say to you, you will by no means come out of there until you have paid the last penny.

Pastor's Reflection

There are passages in Scripture that feel like a gentle invitation—and then there are passages that feel like Jesus has placed His hand directly on your chest, stopping you before you take another step. Matthew 5:21–26 is one of those passages.

I remember when our church entered this section of the Sermon on the Mount. We had just walked through the Beatitudes, where Jesus revealed the character of kingdom people: poor in spirit, meek, merciful, pure in heart, peacemakers. He had called us to be salt and light, to live visibly transformed lives in a dark world. And then He turned to address a hidden enemy—one that lives undetected in the quiet corners of the heart.

As we moved into this teaching, it became clear that Jesus wasn't changing the Law so much as uncovering what had been there all along.

He was about to address something far more common—and far more destructive—than most of us expect. Not murder—not violence—not physical harm.

Anger.

Bitterness.

Contempt.

Often it isn't the loud outbursts that do the damage, but the quieter things we learn to live with—hostility we justify, grudges we carry, and the polite "I'm fine" we use to hide a fractured heart.

As I preached these messages, I watched our church walk through something sacred. The Spirit wasn't just revealing truth —He was revealing hearts. Relationships began to heal. Conversations were sought out that had been avoided for years.

People who had been carrying bitterness finally acknowledged its weight. Quiet apologies were offered. Old wounds began to lose their sting.

And what moved me most were the conversations that happened afterward. One person shared with me that they reached out to someone they had wronged years before. When they apologized, the other person responded in disbelief: "I've never had someone apologize like that... why would you do that?" Moments like that reminded me that reconciliation is not only commanded—it is a powerful testimony of the gospel at work in an ordinary life.

And even though I didn't always see the immediate fruit, I witnessed something just as important: a willingness to be honest before God.

Jesus' words are sharp, but they are the kind of sharp that heals. Like a surgeon's hand, they expose what is wrong so that something healthier can begin to grow in its place.

As we worked through the passage together, I began to see that Jesus was speaking about far more than anger. He was uncovering what anger reveals about the heart, the danger of letting bitterness sit untreated, and the seriousness of worship that ignores broken relationships. He was also calling His people to pursue reconciliation with a kind of urgency we often avoid.

As we walked through this section together, I began to see why Jesus placed this teaching immediately after His call to a righteousness that exceeds the Pharisees. Because nothing reveals the difference between external religion and internal transformation like the way we respond to offense.

This passage pushed us to ask not, "What did they do?" but, "What is happening in my heart?" Not, "How do I defend myself?" but, "How do I honor Christ?" It taught us that the way back is always the same—humility, honesty, and reconciliation.

These words from Jesus are not easy to hear, but over time many of us began to realize how freeing they really are. And for many in our church—myself included—they became the beginning of healing.

You Have Heard It Said: The External Command

Jesus begins with a boundary everyone in the crowd already knew well: "You shall not murder." No one argued with that command. It was clear and widely accepted. Most people felt safe standing behind it.

But Jesus wasn't interested in congratulating the crowd for managing to avoid murder. He was interested in exposing the anger beneath the surface.

He takes the command everyone knows and pushes past the surface to the heart behind it. Murder is the fruit—but anger is the seed. The external act may be absent while the internal poison remains.

For many listening that day, this would have come as a shock. To many today, it still is. We are quick to excuse our anger while condemning the anger of others. We justify our bitterness as "processing," our resentment as "caution," our contempt as "honesty."

But Jesus pulls back every layer and says: the judgment begins at the heart level.

He is not lowering the standard—He is raising it and showing that righteousness in God's kingdom goes deeper than simply avoiding the wrong thing.

The Silent Killer: Anger in the Heart

Anger isn't always explosive. More often it settles in quietly. It shows up in distance, coldness, or the silent decision to pull away from someone we've been hurt by.

This is why Jesus warns not only about anger but about the words that flow from an angry heart—specifically the words "Raca" and "You fool." These terms may feel foreign to us today, but in Jesus' culture they carried a sting far deeper than their English equivalents.

"Raca" was an Aramaic insult that went beyond calling someone foolish. It meant *empty-headed, worthless, beneath consideration.* It was a verbal slap meant to strip a person of dignity—an attack on their intelligence, competence, and value. To say "Raca" was to say, *"You don't matter."*

"You fool" (Greek: *moros*, from which we get *moron*) went even deeper. It wasn't about someone's intellect; it was a moral condemnation. It was the kind of label that declared a person spiritually corrupt, beyond redemption, and beneath God's concern. In that culture, calling someone a "fool" was essentially saying, *"You are godless and hopeless."*

Jesus is showing us that contempt—whether whispered or spoken in private—is never a small matter. These words reveal a heart that has already forgotten the image of God in another person.

Jesus is showing us that the tongue reveals the heart long before the hands ever act.

Unresolved anger is a silent killer. It destroys intimacy, poisons community, erodes trust, and severs relationships. Worst of all, it quietly distances us from God.

In one of the messages we preached, we talked about the progression of bitterness:

Hurt → Anger → Bitterness → Resentment → Contempt → Separation

This is the quiet progression of a wounded heart left unmanaged. It begins with hurt and ends in separation—but it doesn't have to stay that way.

Left unchecked, it does not stay hidden. It spreads. It grows. It takes root.

Hebrews 12:15 describes it as a "root of bitterness" that springs up and defiles many. It never stays private. It always spills outward.

Jesus' warning is not just about behavior. It is about spiritual danger. When anger settles into the heart, judgment is no longer connected to an outward action—it is connected to an inward posture.

This is why Jesus intensifies the warning with each escalating description of anger and contempt. The more we devalue others, the further we drift from the heart of the Father.

The Tongue That Wounds: Words Reflecting the Heart

From anger in the heart, Jesus moves to the words that express it. "Raca." "You fool." Words shaped not by truth but by contempt.

The Bible warns again and again about the damage our words can do. Words can kindle fires (James 3), pierce like swords (Proverbs 12), poison like death (Psalm 140), and crush spirits (Proverbs 18). The damage done by our words is rarely accidental; it flows from the condition of the heart. Jesus isn't simply concerned about vocabulary—He is concerned about the heart that produces it.

Words spoken with contempt reveal more about the speaker than the target. They expose a heart misaligned with kingdom love.

Jesus isn't giving us a list of banned vocabulary. He is calling us to examine the heart that produces the words.

The Pharisees viewed righteousness as rule-keeping. Jesus views righteousness as heart-keeping.

Our words will always betray the true condition of our souls.

Interrupted Worship: Reconciliation Over Ritual

Perhaps the most startling part of this passage is what Jesus says about worship.

"If you bring your gift to the altar and there remember that your brother has something against you..."

In other words, if you are in the act of worship—if you are doing something deeply spiritual—and suddenly God brings to mind a fractured relationship, Jesus says: **stop.**

Don't finish the song. Don't push through the moment.

Stop.

Leave the gift at the altar.

Go to your brother.

Be reconciled.

Then return to worship.

Here is the shocking truth: God prioritizes reconciliation over ritual.

Worship is not merely what happens on a stage, in a song, or in a sanctuary. It is the overflow of a heart aligned with the heart of the Father. And the Father is not pleased with worship offered from a heart harboring bitterness.

Jesus is showing us that unresolved conflict disrupts true worship.

We often think reconciliation is optional, something noble but not necessary. Jesus thinks otherwise. He refuses to separate love for God from love for neighbor.

In this moment, Jesus reveals what kingdom worship looks like—a heart willing to pursue peace, even when it's costly.

Settle It Quickly: The Urgency of Making Things Right

Jesus ends this section with a sense of urgency.

"Agree with your adversary quickly while you are on the way with him..."

Unresolved conflict rarely improves with time. More often it grows deeper and harder to repair.

Jesus isn't providing legal advice—He is providing spiritual wisdom. Settle the matter quickly, because delay gives the enemy room to work.

Reconciliation is rarely convenient. But according to Jesus, it is essential.

Unresolved conflict rarely stays contained. It damages our witness before a watching world, making our faith seem hollow or inconsistent. It hinders our prayers, creating a barrier in our communion with God. It infects our relationships, spreading tension into places that had nothing to do with the original hurt. It steals our joy, replacing peace with heaviness. And it disrupts our worship, dulling our ability to draw near to God with an honest and open heart.

This is why Jesus urges us to settle matters quickly. Delay allows bitterness to grow roots. Quick obedience opens the path to healing.

Jesus is leading us away from a life trapped in bitterness and toward the freedom that comes when we finally let go of old wounds. When Jesus says, “Settle it quickly,” He is not merely giving us a command; He is offering us a path back to peace.

“Settle it quickly” is an invitation into life as it was meant to be lived—where relationships are restored, burdens are lifted, and the heart is no longer chained to old wounds. It is a call to step out of the shadows of resentment and into the healing light of reconciliation.

The Way Back: Humility, Honesty, and Healing

In these verses, Jesus invites us to take an honest look at our hearts. He calls us to let the Spirit reveal what lies beneath the surface, to guard our words carefully because they can wound or restore, to pursue reconciliation instead of letting pride widen the divide, and to come before God in worship with a heart that is seeking peace rather than clinging to bitterness.

The way back from anger and bitterness is always the same path: humility and repentance. This is the very spirit of meekness from the Beatitudes—not weakness, but strength under God’s control. It means choosing not to defend ourselves, not to rehearse old grievances, and not to wait for the other person to make the first move. Instead, Jesus calls us to respond with humility, honesty, initiative, and peacemaking—the very identity He gave His disciples when He said, “Blessed are the peacemakers.” This posture opens the door for real healing and puts the Beatitudes into action in our relationships.

This is the kingdom way—the path that leads to life, where the heart is freed from the weight of anger, relationships are restored, worship is unhindered, and the peace of Christ begins to shape how we treat one another.

Reflection & Practice

Before you move on from this chapter, pause long enough to let Jesus' words search your heart. This is not a passage to skim. It is an invitation to step into honesty, humility, and healing. Let the Spirit guide you as you reflect and respond:

- **What unresolved anger or bitterness is Jesus bringing to mind?**
  Are you holding onto something He is calling you to release? What would it look like to surrender that hurt to Him today?

- **Are there words you've spoken—recently or long ago—that revealed contempt rather than Christlikeness?**
  How might God be inviting you to confess, apologize, or speak life where your words once wounded?

- **Is there someone you need to pursue for reconciliation?**
  Not when it's convenient. Not when the emotion fades. But *quickly*, as Jesus commands. What is one concrete step you can take this week?

- **How might restoring a relationship restore your worship?**
  Jesus connects reconciliation with worship. Where might God be calling you to make peace so that your worship flows freely again?

Take time to pray through these questions. Write down names. Make plans. Seek the Spirit's help. The way back may feel vulnerable—but it is the doorway into freedom, peace, and the life Jesus intends for His people.

Chapter 5

The Look That Lingers: Purity, Desire, and the War Within

Matthew 5:27–30

27 You have heard that it was said by the ancients, "You shall not commit adultery."

28 But I say to you that whoever looks on a woman to lust after her has committed adultery with her already in his heart.

29 And if your right eye causes you to sin, pluck it out and throw it away. For it is profitable that one of your members should perish, and not that your whole body be thrown into hell.

30 And if your right hand causes you to sin, cut it off and throw it away. For it is profitable for you that one of your members should perish, and not that your whole body be thrown into hell.

Pastor's Reflection

Before writing a single word of this chapter, I need to be honest: few passages in the Sermon on the Mount weighed on my heart as heavily as Jesus' words on purity and covenant faithfulness. These were not messages I approached casually, nor were they sermons that allowed me to sleep easily in the nights leading up to them.

There were evenings when I lay awake, praying with a nervous ache in my chest. Not because I feared the text—but because I felt the weight of the people who would hear it. I knew these passages would touched deep wounds, private battles, hidden shame, and quiet fractures inside marriages. I knew these words would land differently for each person—some with tears, some with fear or conviction, and others with a deep longing for hope.

The spiritual attacks intensified. It felt as if the enemy recognized the ground we were about to take. Calls came in from couples whose marriages seemed to be unraveling. Confessions surfaced from people who had been hiding in the shadows for years. Homes were suddenly shaken, relationships strained, and hearts burdened. It was no coincidence. The timing was too precise, the pressure too pointed.

These passages demanded more than study. They required prayer, tears, and a shepherd's heart willing to step carefully into sensitive places.

So as we begin this chapter, know this: every word is written with pastoral compassion, prayer, and deep dependence on the Holy Spirit. Jesus' words here are sharp, but they are not meant to wound. They are meant to heal. He exposes what is hidden not to shame us, but to set us free. The same Jesus who speaks with such clarity also walks with gentle mercy.

This is holy ground, and we will walk it slowly, honestly, and with hope.

The Command Beneath the Surface

Jesus begins this section the same way He began the teaching on anger: *"You have heard that it was said..."* He is quoting a command everyone in His audience would have known—*"You shall not commit adultery."*

No one argued with that command. It was clear, serious, and central to the covenant relationship God designed for marriage. But just as with murder, Jesus refuses to let the conversation stay on the surface.

The religious leaders of His day treated righteousness as a fence—so long as you stayed outside the line of physical adultery, you were safe. But Jesus points to something deeper, something far more honest: the door to adultery is opened long before the act.

Lust is not an action—it is a direction.

It is a movement of the heart. A turning of the gaze. A cultivating of desire.

Adultery doesn't begin with betrayal—it begins with a look.

In our culture, this teaching feels closer than ever. Temptation is no longer distant; it shows up in our pockets, on our screens, in advertisements, in everyday conversations, and even in the quiet corners of our thoughts. Lust is not only tolerated—it is marketed.

But Jesus is calling His followers to something different—a better, whole way of living.

He is not focused on outward appearances; He is focused on inward affections. Because purity is not measured merely by what we avoid, but by what we desire.

The Look That Lingers: When Desire Becomes Devouring

A passing glance is not what Jesus is talking about here. Humans notice beauty—that is not sin. But Jesus speaks of the look that *lingers*—the look that becomes intention, that stirs desire, that imagines what God has forbidden.

Jesus is describing a heart that chooses to entertain what the eyes discover.

Lust turns people into objects and pulls desire away from covenant. What God designed for faithful love becomes something self-centered and self-indulgent. And left unchecked, the look that lingers becomes a look that enslaves.

Temptation usually grows in the heart through a slow progression, often unnoticed until it has already taken root. It unfolds in a predictable way:

- **A glance** becomes **a gaze.**
- **A gaze** becomes **a meditation.**
- **A meditation** becomes **a craving.**
- **A craving** becomes **a decision.**
- **A decision** becomes **destruction.**

Sin rarely starts with a leap—it starts with a look. Temptation slips in quietly, disguised as curiosity, appreciation, or a momentary wandering of the mind. But that small look becomes a doorway, and if left unchecked, a subtle shift begins inside the heart. One lingering thought becomes a pattern, and that pattern becomes a pull. By the time the sin is fully visible, the heart has already traveled a long distance.

Jesus is not interested in behavior modification; He is interested in heart transformation. He isn't saying, "Try harder" or "Just stop it." He is saying, "Guard your desires." He knows that desire shapes direction, and direction shapes decisions. When the heart entertains something long enough, it eventually pursues it. This is why Jesus presses the conversation inward—not to shame us, but to save us from the slow drift that leads to destruction.

Heart Surgery, Not Amputation

Jesus' imagery about plucking out an eye or cutting off a hand is intentionally shocking. But He is not advocating self-mutilation. He is exposing the seriousness of the battle.

Sin cannot be managed—it must be cut off at the root. Jesus is using extreme language to reveal an extreme reality: if something leads you toward sin, you cannot flirt with it, negotiate with it, or keep it at arm's length. You must remove the pathway entirely.

This is not about literal amputation. It is about spiritual surgery. It is about uprooting the things that lead our hearts astray.

This kind of spiritual surgery may require ending a relationship that is pulling you toward compromise or installing new boundaries that guard your eyes and thoughts. It may mean seeking accountability instead of continuing in secrecy. It could involve changing the habits, routines, or environments that continually open the door to temptation. And at times, it may require confronting hidden patterns you've been ignoring for far too long. **Jesus is not calling us to harm our bodies—He is calling us to dismantle whatever nurtures our sin.**

As temptation loses its footing, freedom begins to take root. Jesus is not trying to shame us into change—He is trying to free us from chains we have carried for far too long. And He reminds us of something we often forget: sin grows in silence, but it dies in the light.

Wholly Committed: Purity Flows From Devotion

Before Jesus ever talks about divorce, He roots the conversation in purity. This is because purity and covenant faithfulness are connected.

A heart that is divided in desire becomes a heart divided in devotion.

Purity is not merely the absence of lust; it is the presence of wholehearted commitment. It is loving one person faithfully. It is honoring the covenant God designed. It is choosing a life shaped not by fleeting desire but by lasting faithfulness.

This is why the call to purity is not simply about resisting temptation—it is about redirecting affection. The more our hearts are captivated by Christ, the less room they have for counterfeit desires.

When our hearts are filled with the beauty of who Jesus is, sinful desires lose their appeal.

The War Within: Desire, Discipline, and Dependence

Purity does not come from white-knuckled willpower, and lust is not defeated by determination alone. Jesus is not calling us to self-reliance—He is calling us to Spirit-dependence.

The battle for purity is won not only through discipline but through desire. This is the very heartbeat of Jesus' Beatitude: *"Blessed are the pure in heart, for they shall see God."* We pursue purity by pursuing Him—by inviting Him to reshape our affections, reorder our loves, and renew our minds, so that our desires align with the kind of heart that sees and treasures God above all else.

This is why Jesus' teaching here is not simply a warning; it is also an invitation into freedom.

He exposes the war within so that He can lead us to victory.

And victory is possible—not because we are strong, but because He is.

Reflection & Practice

Before you leave this chapter, take time to let Jesus' words settle deeply. Purity is not a destination—it is a direction. It is the ongoing shaping of the heart by the Spirit of God. Let these questions guide your reflection:

- **Where have your eyes or thoughts lingered in ways that pull your heart away from purity?**
  What desires is Jesus inviting you to surrender into His hands?

- **Are there pathways to temptation that need to be removed rather than managed?**
  What "heart surgery" might Jesus be calling you to pursue in this season? Are there habits, environments, or patterns that need to be cut off at the root?

- **How does your pursuit of purity reflect your devotion to Christ—and, if married, your covenant commitment?**
  In what ways might Jesus be inviting you to love more faithfully, guard your heart more intentionally, or realign your affections more fully with His design?

- **Where do you need to exchange self-reliance for Spirit-dependence?**
  What would it look like to invite the Holy Spirit into your desires—not just your discipline—and trust Him to reshape the inner life of your heart?

Take time to pray honestly. Confess freely. Surrender willingly. Purity is not about perfection—it is about direction. And the direction Jesus leads always moves toward freedom, wholeness, and life.

Chapter 6
Wholly Committed: Faithfulness in a Fractured World

Matthew 5:31-32

31 It was said, "Whoever divorces his wife, let him give her a certificate of divorce."

32 But I say to you that whoever divorces his wife, except for marital unfaithfulness, causes her to commit adultery. And whoever marries her who is divorced commits adultery.

Pastor's Reflection

When we came to Jesus' words on marriage and divorce, the weight I felt was different from the weight of the previous passage. The purity texts pressed heavily on individual hearts—but these verses focused in on homes and families, on stories that stretch across years. This wasn't the weight of hidden battles—it was the weight of public wounds, long histories, and deep relational fractures.

The nights leading up to this passage weren't marked by fear or dread but by a kind of solemn awareness. I knew I would be speaking into the living rooms of people whose marriages were fragile, strained, and sometimes simply exhausted. I knew I'd be talking to believers carrying decades of regret or confusion. I knew divorced brothers and sisters would hear these words through tears—some from hurt, others from healing, and some from shame the church has not always handled well.

Before preaching these messages, I remember praying with a unique kind of tenderness. Not nervousness this time, but a pastoral sensitivity—"Lord, help me speak with the same balance Jesus uses here: truth without harshness, compassion without compromise."

And right as we reached this point in the Sermon on the Mount, marriages around us *did* come under pressure. Not in the same way as before—this time it wasn't temptation or secrecy, but discouragement, hopelessness, and the slow erosion that happens when two hearts drift. Phone calls came not with shock but with sorrow. Couples weren't confessing hidden sins—they were expressing quiet collapse.

That reminded me of something: **marriages often break long before they shatter**. And Jesus' words here are meant to catch us in the *cracks* before we reach the breaking point.

So as you read this chapter, know this: these words are written with compassion for the divorced and hope for those still fighting for their marriages. Jesus' teaching here is not meant to reopen old wounds—it is meant to guide us toward healing, clarity, and covenant faithfulness.

This is tender ground. And we will walk it gently, honestly, and with the Shepherd who restores souls.

The Ancient Debate: What Jesus Was Addressing

To understand Jesus' words, we must understand the world He was speaking into. In His day, there was a raging debate between two major rabbinic schools:

- **Shammai**, who taught divorce was only permitted for sexual immorality.

- **Hillel**, who taught divorce could be granted for almost anything—spoiled food, a raised voice, or a wife who was "less pleasing" than another woman.

The culture Jesus spoke into had normalized divorce. It was casual, convenient, and often cruel. Men dismissed their wives with little thought for the devastation left behind.

So when Jesus speaks, He speaks into a world where covenant faithfulness was already crumbling.

And He does not soften His tone.

The Heart of the Matter: Covenant, Not Convenience

When Jesus says, *"Whoever divorces his wife, except for sexual immorality, causes her to commit adultery,"* He is not simply tightening religious regulations. He is restoring covenant to its God-given weight.

Marriage was never meant to be a contract of convenience. It was designed to be a covenant of commitment—one that reflects the faithfulness of God toward His people.

Covenant says:

- *"I will love you faithfully."*
- *"I will stay when it's difficult."*
- *"I will choose you repeatedly."*
- *"I will honor God in how I honor you."*

Jesus is pulling marriage out of the hands of culture and placing it back into the hands of the Creator.

Marriage was never meant to be disposable. And divorce was never meant to be easy.

When the Covenant Breaks: The Pain of Sexual Immorality

Jesus gives one clear exception—sexual immorality. When one spouse violates the covenant through unfaithfulness, the marriage bond is torn in a unique and devastating way.

Sexual immorality is not merely a mistake—it is a breach of the deepest form of trust. It wounds at a level words cannot fully capture, shattering safety, fracturing intimacy, and breaking what was meant to be guarded.

Jesus acknowledges the profound damage caused by betrayal. He does not *command* divorce—but He *permits* it, recognizing the severity of the harm.

And yet, even here, restoration, redemption, and healing are possible. Many marriages have risen from this kind of wreckage by the power of forgiveness and grace.

But Jesus refuses to pretend the wound is small.

Abandonment and Destruction: What Paul Later Clarifies

Paul later adds clarity to situations Jesus did not directly address — specifically, **abandonment** (1 Corinthians 7:15). When an unbelieving spouse deserts the marriage, the believing spouse is "not bound."

Abandonment is more than physical departure. It can take many forms:

- **Refusing to provide** — withdrawing the basic support a spouse is responsible to give.
- **Persistent neglect** — habitually withholding care, partnership, or presence.
- **Chronic abuse** — using harm, fear, or control in ways that violate covenant love.
- **Destructive addiction** — repeatedly choosing a substance or behavior over the marriage despite calls to change.

- **A refusal to live as a covenant partner** — rejecting the responsibilities, commitments, and unity that marriage requires.

These forms of abandonment reflect situations where a spouse has functionally deserted the marriage, even if not physically absent — a principle consistent with Paul's teaching in 1 Corinthians 7:15.

Paul acknowledges that while God hates divorce, God does not require a spouse to remain in a marriage where the other partner has already abandoned the covenant in every meaningful way.

This creates two biblical grounds for divorce:

1. **Sexual immorality** (Matthew 5:32).
2. **Abandonment** (1 Corinthians 7:15).

Scripture's goal is not to trap people in destruction—it is to honor covenant and protect the vulnerable.

The Impact of Divorce: A Wound with Many Layers

Divorce is always painful; even when biblically permitted, it is a tearing—not a clean break. It affects:

- spouses
- children
- extended family
- friendships
- finances

- spiritual and emotional health

It leaves questions, fears, grief, and sometimes guilt.

And yet, Scripture does not treat divorced people as second-class. God does not discard those who have been hurt by broken covenants. Jesus meets the wounded with compassion, not condemnation.

The church must reflect the same heart.

Building Strong Homes in a Fractured World

If the enemy destroys the home, generations are disrupted. But when Christ strengthens the home, the future grows stronger.

So how do we build marriages that endure?

1. Commitment Before Emotion

Feelings rise and fall. Commitment anchors the marriage when emotions fluctuate.

2. Communication Rooted in Truth and Grace

Honest conversations. Gentle words. Forgiving spirits.

3. Sacrificial Love

Love that serves rather than demands. Love that mirrors Christ.

4. Mutual Submission

Not dominance—but shared humility. Respect. Partnership.

5. Christ at the Center

When both spouses move toward Christ, they inevitably move closer to each other.

Strong homes do not happen by accident. They are built intentionally, prayerfully, and with daily choices that honor the covenant.

Reflection & Practice

Let Jesus' words on covenant and faithfulness guide your heart as you reflect:

- **How does Jesus' teaching challenge your view of marriage or divorce?**
  Where is He calling you to deeper understanding or healing?

- **Is there a place where covenant faithfulness is being tested in your life?**
  What steps toward restoration, repentance, or reconciliation may be needed?

- **How can you strengthen your home (or future home) with intentional practices of love, communication, and devotion to Christ?**

- **If you carry wounds from divorce—your own or someone else's—how is Jesus inviting you into healing, grace, and hope?**

Take these questions slowly. Let the Holy Spirit speak tenderly. Covenant faithfulness is not a burden—it is a blessing. And Christ Himself is faithful to restore what has been broken, heal what has been wounded, and strengthen what remains fragile.

Chapter 7
Let Your Yes Be Yes

Matthew 5:33–37

33 Again, you have heard that it was said by the ancients, "You shall not swear falsely, but shall fulfill your oaths to the Lord."

34 But I say to you, do not swear at all: neither by heaven, for it is God's throne;

35 Nor by the earth, for it is His footstool; nor by Jerusalem, for it is the city of the great King.

36 Nor shall you swear by your head, because you cannot make one hair white or black.

37 But let your 'Yes' mean 'Yes,' and 'No' mean 'No.' For whatever is more than these comes from the evil one.

Pastor's Reflection

When I first studied Jesus' words about oaths, promises, and integrity, something different happened in my heart. Not the heaviness of grief or urgency that comes with topics like anger, purity, or marriage—but a steady, quiet conviction that reached into the ordinary corners of life. It clarified something essential about discipleship: **following Jesus transforms not only our big decisions but the everyday words we speak without thinking.**

What struck me most wasn't hypocrisy—it was recognition. Recognition that even sincere people—people who love Jesus, who want to live faithfully—can slip into careless commitments, casual exaggerations, or well-intentioned promises they struggle to keep. Integrity is rarely shattered in dramatic moments; it usually erodes in small, unnoticed ways.

As I studied this passage, the Spirit brought to mind the small conversations and quick assurances we often make without thinking about the weight behind them. And I realized how deeply Jesus cares about even these small places.

Because for Jesus, this isn't about dramatic oaths or courtroom vows. It's about becoming the kind of person who doesn't need extra words to be believed. A person whose commitments carry weight because their character is trustworthy. A person whose "yes" means yes simply because it comes from a trustworthy heart. It's about the kind of life where people don't need to question what you mean—because your character has spoken long before your mouth has.

The Old Problem: Using Words to Avoid Truth

In Jesus' day, people had developed elaborate systems for making promises. Some oaths were binding. Others were not. Swear by the temple? Binding. Swear by the gold of the temple? More binding. Swear by heaven? Not quite binding. Swear by the throne of God? Definitely binding.

It had become a maze of words, carefully arranged so people could avoid truth while still sounding honest.

The Pharisees had created a culture where you could sound honest without actually being honest. As long as you phrased your words cleverly, you could give the impression of integrity while leaving yourself a loophole big enough to walk away.

Jesus steps into that culture and cuts through the fog: **"Do not swear at all."**

He's not forbidding wedding vows or legal promises. He's confronting a dishonest heart that uses religious language to mask unreliable character.

Integrity Without Layers

Jesus' command is simple: *"Let your 'Yes' be 'Yes' and your 'No,' 'No.'"* He is calling His people to a life where truth is clear, straightforward, and trustworthy.

When your words are consistent, your character is credible.

We shouldn't need verbal padding or spiritual-sounding formulas to convince others we mean what we say. The people of God should speak with such integrity that our simple "yes" carries the weight of a vow—and our simple "no" is received without suspicion.

In a world where language is often used to manipulate, exaggerate, or conceal, Jesus calls us to be different—to live with integrity that is unlayered, uncomplicated, and unmistakable.

This is not just about what we promise—it is about the kind of people we are becoming. Integrity shows up in the small places long before it is tested in the large ones. It looks like honesty in ordinary conversations, consistency in the way we interact with others day after day, reliability in the commitments we make, and freedom from the subtle forms of manipulation that creep into our speech when we want to be admired or avoid discomfort. These seemingly small choices shape the kind of character that does not need extra words to prove anything. Integrity is built not by dramatic moments of resolve but through countless quiet decisions to speak truthfully, simply, and without pretense.

The Heart Behind the Words

Jesus isn't primarily addressing vocabulary—He's addressing *integrity*. The issue isn't swearing an oath; it's needing to swear an oath to be believed.

The deeper question is this: Why would someone need to strengthen their words?

When Jesus challenges our need to strengthen our words, He is inviting us to consider why that need arises at all. For many, it is because their life has not been consistently aligned with their speech—others have learned to doubt what they say. For some, it is the residue of promises made too quickly or commitments taken on without the follow-through to sustain them. And for others, it is a subtle desire to be perceived as more reliable, more spiritual, or more impressive than the truth would naturally reveal. Jesus is exposing these quiet motivations so that our words can flow from an honest and steady life rather than from a need to manage perceptions.

But the kingdom Jesus describes is one where the inside matches the outside. Where truth is not embellished. Where words and actions align.

Integrity begins in the heart, long before it ever becomes visible in the words we speak.

Integrity in an Exaggerated World

We live in a culture addicted to exaggeration. Words like "always," "never," "best ever," and "worst ever" fill our conversations. Social media celebrates polished versions of ourselves, and everyday speech drifts toward dramatization.

Jesus calls us back to simple honesty.

The words of a disciple should create an atmosphere of trust wherever they are spoken. They should carry humility—never inflated with self-importance or shaped by a need to impress and should avoid the exaggeration that our culture so easily accepts. Choosing instead the grounded honesty that reflects a heart anchored in truth. And above all, our words should honor God, revealing a character shaped not by haste or impulse but by the presence of the Holy Spirit within us. When our speech carries these qualities, our conversations become a witness to the reliability and faithfulness of the God we serve.

When we refuse to dress up the truth—or twist it slightly for benefit—we reflect the God who **never lies**, and whose Word is always trustworthy.

The Enemy of Integrity: Self-Justification

Jesus warns that anything beyond "yes" and "no" comes "from the evil one." That sounds severe—until you understand what He means.

Whenever we try to justify ourselves, inflate our words, or manipulate how others perceive us, we step onto dangerous ground. We are tempted to imitate the serpent in the garden, who used deceptive language to distort truth.

Self-justification is subtle, and it often grows quietly in the spaces where we feel insecure or misunderstood. It shows up when we excuse small compromises as insignificant, forgetting that those compromises shape who we are becoming. It reveals itself when we use our words to carefully protect our reputation rather than confessing honestly where we have fallen short. And it appears when we craft sentences that allow us convenient escape routes—commitments we can back away from later without technically lying. These habits may seem harmless, but Jesus knows they erode integrity from the inside out. He calls His people not merely to avoid falsehood but to walk in the freedom that comes from truthfulness without defensiveness.

Jesus wants to free us from all of that.

Integrity does not need defending, because it stands on its own.

A Life Where Words and Character Align

Jesus is not merely correcting our words—He is inviting us into a life that has been transformed. It is a life in which It is a life in which your words are so steady, so sincere, that people never have to analyze or decode them. It is a life where your commitments are honored with quiet faithfulness, where your reputation is shaped by long obedience rather than momentary impressions, and where your honesty becomes a quiet gift to the people who trust you. In this kind of life, your speech is simple, sincere, and unforced—free from the embellishments we use to impress and the evasions we use to protect ourselves. It is a life where integrity itself becomes a testimony, speaking louder than any oath could, because your words reflect a character shaped by the God whose promises are always true.

But this kind of life doesn't appear out of nowhere. It flows directly from the Beatitudes—the very character Jesus has been forming in His disciples since the beginning of this sermon.

Integrity is what happens when the Beatitudes move from belief

into practice.

When you are *poor in spirit*, you have no need to exaggerate your importance.

When you *mourn over sin*, you refuse to cover it with excuses.

When you walk in *meekness*, you don't use words to dominate or manipulate.

When you *hunger and thirst for righteousness*, truth—not image—becomes your pursuit.

When you are *pure in heart*, your words are clean because your motives are clean.

When you are a *peacemaker*, your speech becomes a tool for healing, not division.

When you endure *persecution for righteousness' sake*, you stand firm in truth even when it costs you.

In other words, integrity is **the outward evidence of a heart shaped by the Beatitudes.** When the character Jesus describes begins to take root inside us, it naturally begins to show up in the way we speak, the promises we make, and the truthfulness of our lives.

This kind of life may seem quiet, but over time it becomes unmistakable—because it reflects the character of the Father whose promises never fail.

Reflection & Practice

Let Jesus' call to integrity search and strengthen your heart:

- **Where do your words tend to stretch beyond the truth—intentionally or unintentionally?**
  Where might Jesus be inviting you to greater honesty?

- **Are there commitments you've made that need to be revisited, clarified, or fulfilled?**
  Integrity is strengthened through follow-through.

- **Do people who know you best trust your words?**
  What would it look like to grow in reliability and consistency?

- **Is there an area where you've used language to justify yourself, soften a truth, or protect your image?**
  Bring it into the light. Jesus is faithful to both forgive and reshape.

Take time to slow down, reflect, and listen. Integrity is not about perfection—it's about alignment. And Jesus is forming in you a heart where your "yes" is trustworthy, your "no" is steady, and your words reflect the truthfulness of the God you follow.

Chapter 8
The Second Mile: Love That Goes Further

Matthew 5:38–48

38 You have heard that it was said, "An eye for an eye, and a tooth for a tooth."

39 But I say to you, do not resist an evil person. But whoever strikes you on your right cheek, turn to him the other as well.

40 And if anyone sues you in a court of law and takes away your tunic, let him have your cloak also.

41 And whoever compels you to go a mile, go with him two.

42 Give to him who asks you, and from him who would borrow from you do not turn away.

43 You have heard that it was said, "You shall love your neighbor and hate your enemy."

44 But I say to you, love your enemies, bless those who curse you, do good to those who hate you, and pray for those who spitefully use you and persecute you,

45 That you may be sons of your Father who is in heaven. For He makes His sun rise on the evil and on the good and sends rain on the just and on the unjust.

46 For if you love those who love you, what reward do you have? Do not even the tax collectors do the same?

47 And if you greet your brothers only, what are you doing more than others? Do not even the tax collectors do so?

48 Therefore be perfect, even as your Father who is in heaven is perfect.

Pastor's Reflection

Some passages comfort and some confront—but this one exposes the heart in a way that is hard to ignore. Jesus' call to radical generosity, unexpected grace, and enemy love is one of the clearest windows into the heart of God—and one of the sharpest mirrors held up to the human soul.

When I first studied this section, it was the *simplicity* of Jesus' words that unsettled me. Not because they were confusing, but because they were unmistakably clear. There is no way to soften them, no loophole to hide in, no cultural explanation that makes them easier. Jesus is not giving us suggestions; He is revealing the character of the kingdom.

And He is revealing the character of the King.

As I prayed through these verses, I remember feeling the weight of what happens when grace goes further than expected. There is something powerful when believers respond to mistreatment with kindness, when generosity refuses to be calculated, and when love crosses the very lines the world draws.

I also thought about what could happen in our church as we grow into this teaching—how powerful it might be when believers choose grace over retaliation, when second-mile love softens hardened hearts, and when forgiveness creates healing where wounds once defined relationships.

Jesus' words here are not a call to passivity. They reveal a kingdom that refuses to mirror retaliation or live under resentment—a kingdom that loves differently because its people belong to a different King.

This chapter is an invitation to step into that kind of life—a life that goes further than what is fair, expected, or deserved.

The First Mile: Powerless Obligation

When Jesus says, *"Whoever compels you to go one mile, go with him two,"* His listeners immediately understood the reference. Roman soldiers could legally force a Jewish man to carry their gear for one mile. It was degrading, unjust, and humiliating. The first mile was not a choice—it was oppression.

Everyone hated it.

And Jesus says: *"Go further."*

This is where the kingdom of God diverges sharply from the kingdoms of men. The world asks, *"What is the least I can do?"* Jesus asks, *"What would love do?"*

In the first mile, you walk because you must. You have no control, no choice, no dignity in the exchange. But in the second mile, you take control back—not by force, but by grace.

The second mile is where bitterness begins to dissolve and dignity returns, where wounds take on new meaning and unexpected conversations begin.

The Roman soldier may command the first mile—but only the disciple can offer the second.

The Second Mile: Radical Generosity

Jesus applies the same principle to real situations—insults, lawsuits, forced service, and unexpected requests. In each, He moves the disciple from **reaction** to **redemption**.

1. Turn the other cheek

In the ancient Jewish world, a slap on the **right cheek** was almost always a **backhanded slap**—the most insulting gesture a person could deliver. It wasn't an act of violence meant to injure; it was an insult meant to shame. Jesus is not telling His followers to remain in abusive situations; He is telling them not to respond to **insult with insult**, or to let someone else's contempt produce bitterness in their own soul.

Turning the other cheek is the courage to meet insult without imitating it. It is the strength to remain steady when someone tries to provoke you. It is the freedom to say, *"Your attempt to diminish me will not define me—my dignity comes from God."*

2. Give more than demanded

In Jewish law, a person's **cloak** (outer garment) was essential—so essential that even if taken as collateral, it had to be returned before sundown. It was a person's warmth, shelter, and protection. When Jesus says, *"If anyone takes your tunic, let him have your cloak also,"* He is speaking shocking generosity into a culture where the cloak was a legal right.

Jesus isn't commanding recklessness with personal safety; He is illustrating a heart so free from retaliation and self-preservation that it can release even what is legally protected. It is a picture of a disciple whose identity is anchored not in possessions or protections, but in the Father's care.

3. Go the second mile

The second mile was where everything changed. The first mile was forced, humiliating, and imposed by Roman law—but the second mile belonged entirely to the disciple. It was an unexpected act of grace, a choice so unusual that it demanded explanation. The second mile transformed a degrading command into a holy opportunity—an opportunity to reveal a different kingdom and a different kind of King. It disrupted the cycle of hostility and opened the door for conversations, curiosity, and even the softening of hardened hearts. It showed that the kingdom of God does not advance through power or resentment, but through willing, surprising, self-giving love.

4. Give to those who ask

This final example captures the posture of a heart shaped by the generosity of God. "Give to those who ask" is not a call to reckless irresponsibility, but to a readiness to meet needs without clinging to possessions or self-protection. Jesus invites His followers to see requests not as interruptions but as opportunities—to reflect the Father who gives daily bread to the grateful and ungrateful alike. This kind of generosity is slow, thoughtful, open-handed, and Spirit-led. It reveals a heart that trusts God more than it fears lack.

Generosity in the kingdom of God is not measured by calculation, but by compassion.

In every case, Jesus is forming a people who are unoffendable, unselfish, unthreatened, and unshakably anchored in the Father's care.

And all of this—the cheek, the cloak, the mile—flows directly from the **Beatitudes**:

Only the meek can refuse to retaliate.
Only the merciful can release what is rightfully theirs.
Only the pure in heart can give without hidden motives.
Only the peacemakers can walk the second mile with grace.
Only those willing to face persecution can love beyond what the world considers fair .

These teachings are not random commands—they are the practical outworking of a Beatitude-shaped heart.

Love Past the Line

The most shocking part of this passage is not the second mile—it is the command to *love your enemies.* Jesus replaces the cultural rule —love your neighbor, tolerate your enemy—with the kingdom rule:

love both.

This is not theoretical. Jesus' instructions move from outward response to inward transformation—speaking blessing instead of curses, doing good where harm was expected, and praying for those who cause pain. These are not tasks on a list but movements of the heart. You cannot pray honestly for someone and continue hating them; prayer softens what bitterness hardens.

Enemy love is not a sentimental feeling—it is a Christ-shaped choice, and often the hardest one Jesus calls His followers to make.

Why Enemy Love Matters

Jesus gives the reason plainly: *"that you may be sons of your Father who is in heaven."*

Loving enemies is not how we *become* God's children—it is how God's children show who their Father is.

God loves in a way that is impartial and surprising. He pours out sunlight and rain—symbols of His provision—on those who honor Him and those who ignore Him. Every day, God displays unearned grace to people who do nothing to deserve it.

When we love enemies, we reflect His heart.

When we cross the lines others draw, we reveal His kingdom.

When we extend grace that makes no sense, we declare that Jesus is Lord.

What More Are You Doing Than Others?

Jesus' question pierces the heart: *"What are you doing more than others?"*

Anyone can love the lovable. Anyone can greet their friends. Anyone can be kind to those who agree with them.

But disciples go further.

Because grace went further for them.

The second mile is not about self-improvement but about the kind of transformation the Spirit produces—a life that overflows with the power of the gospel.

The Call to Wholeness

Jesus ends with the most challenging statement in the passage: *"Be perfect, even as your Father in heaven is perfect."*

The word "perfect" here means *complete, mature, whole.* Jesus is not demanding flawless performance—He is calling us to become people whose love is not partial or divided.

To love only friends is incomplete.
To love only family is immature.
To love only people who please us is unfinished.

But to love enemies—
to show grace where none is deserved,
to walk a second mile no one expects—
that is wholeness.

Reflection & Practice

Let these words of Jesus form your heart toward radical, second-mile love:

- **Where is God calling you to go the second mile?**
  In your home? Workplace? Church?

- **When were you last tempted to respond in the "first-mile" way—defending yourself, demanding fairness, or retreating into resentment?**
  How might Jesus be inviting you to respond with grace instead of retaliation?

- **Who is the "enemy" Jesus is calling you to bless, help, or pray for?**
  Not necessarily a sworn enemy—often it is the difficult person, the frustrating relationship, or the one who misunderstands you.

- **Is there someone God is asking you to forgive or serve beyond what feels reasonable?**
  What would the second mile look like in that relationship?

- **Where is the Spirit inviting you to trust the Father's provision instead of clinging to rights, possessions, or emotional defenses?**
  How might generosity or humility reflect the Father's heart in that moment?

Take a moment to sit with these questions. Second-mile love does not come from human strength; it comes from a heart shaped by grace and empowered by the Spirit. As you walk with Jesus, He will give you the strength to go further than expected and to reflect the love of the Father who went further for you.

Chapter 9
The Hidden Life: For the Father's Eyes

Matthew 6:1-18

1 Be sure that you not do your charitable deeds before men to be seen by them. Otherwise you have no reward from your Father who is in heaven.

2 Therefore, when you do your charitable deeds, do not sound a trumpet before you as the hypocrites do in the synagogues and in the streets, that they may be honored by men. Truly I say to you, they have their reward.

3 But when you do your charitable deeds, do not let your left hand know what your right hand is doing,

4 That your charitable deeds may be in secret. And your Father who sees in secret will Himself reward you openly.

5 When you pray, you shall not be like the hypocrites. For they love to pray standing in the synagogues and on the street corners that they may be seen by men. Truly I say to you, they have their reward.

6 But you, when you pray, enter your closet, and when you have shut your door, pray to your Father who is in secret. And your Father who sees in secret will reward you openly.

7 But when you pray, do not use vain repetitions, as the heathen do. For they think that they will be heard for their much speaking.

8 Do not be like them, for your Father knows what things you have need of before you ask Him.

9 Therefore pray in this manner: Our Father who is in heaven, hallowed be Your name.

10 Your kingdom come; Your will be done on earth, as it is in heaven.

11 Give us this day our daily bread.

12 And forgive us our debts, as we forgive our debtors.

13 And lead us not into temptation, but deliver us from evil. For Yours is the kingdom and the power and the glory forever. Amen.

14 For if you forgive men for their sins, your heavenly Father will also forgive you.

15 But if you do not forgive men for their sins, neither will your Father forgive your sins.

16 Moreover, when you fast, do not be like the hypocrites with a sad countenance. For they disfigure their faces so they may appear to men to be fasting. Truly I say to you, they have their reward.

17 But you, when you fast, anoint your head and wash your face,

18 So that you will not appear to men to be fasting, but to your Father who is in secret. And your Father who sees in secret will reward you openly.

Pastor's Reflection

Some passages feel like they whisper. Others feel like they expose. This one does both.

When I first stepped into Matthew 6, I felt a shift—a quiet but unmistakable turn in Jesus' teaching. Matthew 5 had been loud with light, bold with influence, full of public witness: "You are the salt of the earth… you are the light of the world." But now Jesus pivots. Instead of the visible life of the disciple, He brings us into the **hidden** one.

This transition unsettled me—in the best way. It forced me to wrestle not with what people see, but with what God sees. And that is a far more searching evaluation.

During this season of study, I remember how God gently exposed my own heart. Not with condemnation, but with clarity.

So much of our spiritual activity can slowly drift toward performance, comparison, or the subtle desire to be seen by others. We rarely plan for that to happen, and we almost never say it out loud—but over time our motives can begin to mix.

And Jesus, in His mercy, calls us back.

He calls us into the kind of faith where the loudest moments happen in silence, the truest worship happens unnoticed, and the deepest formation happens when no one but the Father is watching.

The hidden life is not a lesser life. In many ways it is the **truest** one—the life where faith is formed quietly before the Father, where motives are purified, and where devotion grows without the need to be seen.

The Call to the Hidden Life

Jesus begins with a warning that strikes the soul: "Beware"—not of persecution or false teaching, but of something far more subtle and far more dangerous: the temptation to do the right things for the wrong eyes.

This is the heartbeat of Matthew 6:1–18. Jesus is not questioning *whether* you give, pray, or fast. He assumes His disciples will do all three. What He examines is the **audience**.

Do we give for God's eyes—or for people's applause?

Do we pray for the Father's reward—or for the impression of spirituality?

Do we fast to draw near to God—or to appear devoted?

When Giving Goes Quiet

Jesus begins with giving—not because it is most important, but because it is most easily twisted.

In His day, religious leaders would literally sound a trumpet to announce their generosity. Today, the trumpet is subtler: strategic timing, public posts, carefully phrased stories, quiet ways of making sure generosity is noticed.

Jesus isn't shaming generosity. He's rescuing it.

He says, in essence: *"Give—but give in such a way that only the Father notices."*

Not to impress. Not to position yourself. Not to build influence. But because the Father delights in generosity born from mercy.

And then Jesus gives one of the most vivid images in the chapter:

"Do not let your left hand know what your right hand is doing." It's a picture of quiet, almost instinctive generosity—giving so sincere it needs no audience but God.

This kind of giving reflects the Beatitudes—the meek who do not seek attention, the merciful who give freely, and the pure in heart whose motives are not mixed.

When Prayer Goes Secret

Jesus then turns to prayer, and His words cut even closer to the heart. Few things reveal our true desires more than the way we pray.

Some prayed on street corners with elevated voices—not to commune with God, but to curate an image. Others used endless repetition, believing that God could be impressed or manipulated by volume.

Jesus cuts through all of it: *"When you pray, go into your room and shut the door."*

This is not about avoiding public prayer; it's about avoiding public performance.

Secret prayer strips away the pressure to be seen as spiritual. It removes comparison. It reveals whether we desire God—or just desire to appear godly.

And yet Jesus also gives comfort here: *"Your Father knows what you need before you ask."* Hidden prayer is not unseen prayer. It is prayer seen by the only One whose attention matters.

While Jesus gives the model prayer that follows, His concern is not that we recite the words themselves but that we embody the heart behind them. The Lord's Prayer re-centers us on the Father's holiness, aligns us with His kingdom, reminds us of His provision, calls us to forgive as we have been forgiven, and teaches us to depend on His protection. Even so, the key remains the same: prayer is not a performance to impress others but a sincere posture before the Father who sees in secret.

When Fasting Goes Hidden

And just as giving reveals our motives and prayer tests our desires, fasting uncovers what we hunger for most.

Fasting is one of the disciplines most easily turned into display. In the first century, many religious leaders chose to fast on Mondays and Thursdays—the busiest market days in Jerusalem—when the crowds were largest and the temptation to *be noticed* was strongest. Many even exaggerated their appearance—leaving themselves unkempt or dramatizing their discomfort—to ensure others recognized their devotion. Their goal wasn't communion with God but admiration from people.

Jesus dismantles the entire performance with a simple command: *"Anoint your head and wash your face."*

In other words: *"Look normal. Don't advertise your sacrifice."*

True fasting is not about appearing holy—it is about redirecting hunger toward God, allowing physical desire to awaken deeper spiritual longing.

And again, the same refrain: **"Your Father who sees in secret will reward you."** The reward is not the admiration of others; the reward is God Himself.

The Father Who Sees

The refrain of the chapter is unmistakable: your Father *sees in secret,* your Father *knows,* and your Father *rewards.*

Jesus grounds every act of hidden devotion in the relationship His disciples have with God as their Father. The hidden life is not built on fear but on belonging. It grows from the quiet confidence that we do not perform for God—we walk with Him. We do not earn His attention—we already have it.

with Him. We do not earn His attention—we already *have* it.

When Jesus speaks of secrecy, He is not pushing us into isolation but drawing us into deeper communion, where our motives are purified and our love is clarified.

In the hidden place, there is no stage, no audience, no pressure to impress. There is only the Father who delights in *sincerity,* who shapes us in the *quiet,* and who rewards what no one else ever sees.

This is why secrecy becomes a form of freedom: it delivers us from the exhausting cycle of comparison and reminds us that nothing done for God is ever unnoticed by Him.

Children do not need an audience when they are with their Father *—His attention is enough.*

Reflection & Practice

The hidden life cannot be rushed, measured, or displayed. It grows slowly in the quiet spaces where only God sees. Before you move on, take a moment to let these truths settle. Ask the Spirit to expose where motives have drifted, to quiet the noise of comparison, and to strengthen your desire to be seen by the Father alone.

Transformation in the hidden places always begins with honest reflection.

Let the hidden life shape your heart this week:

- **Where are you tempted to seek approval or recognition in your spiritual life?**
  What would it look like to offer that area back to God alone?

- **How is God inviting you to practice one discipline—giving, praying, or fasting—in secret this week?**
  What small step of hidden devotion could you take?

- **Is there a place where comparison has silently crept into your walk with Christ?**
  How might secret worship quiet that noise?

Chapter 10
The Heart Test, The Eye Test, & The Master Test

Matthew 6:19-24

19 Do not store up for yourselves treasures on earth, where moth and rust destroy and where thieves break in and steal.

20 But store up for yourselves treasures in heaven, where neither moth nor rust destroys and where thieves do not break in nor steal.

21 For where your treasure is, there will your heart be also.

22 The light of the body is the eye. Therefore, if your eye is clear, your whole body will be full of light.

23 But if your eye is bad, your whole body will be full of darkness. If therefore the light that is in you is darkness, how great is that darkness!

24 No one can serve two masters. For either he will hate the one and love the other, or he will be devoted to the one and despise the other. You cannot serve God and money.

Pastor's Reflection

While preparing these messages from Matthew 6:19–24, I had the uncomfortable sense that Jesus was holding an x-ray up to my own heart. Things I hadn't noticed before suddenly came into focus—what I treasure, what shapes my attention, and what quietly competes for my loyalty.

As I prepared these messages, I discovered that Jesus wasn't simply warning about money or possessions. He was calling His disciples into a deeper examination—a searching of the heart that presses beyond behavior and reaches into desire, focus, and loyalty. These words did not merely instruct me; they searched me.

The longer I sat with the passage, the more it began to surface uncomfortable questions. Questions like: *What do I really treasure? What quietly shapes my choices? What has more of my attention than I realize?* These questions didn't accuse—they invited. They invited me into freedom, into clarity, into loyalty that is unburdened and undivided.

These verses follow naturally from the hidden life Jesus described earlier, forming the next layer of His invitation into an inner life shaped by the Father. Once our motives are purified before the Father's eyes, Jesus turns next to examine what fills our hearts, directs our vision, and commands our allegiance. This passage is not about money alone—it is about the shape of our inner life.

Through this passage Jesus quietly lays out three tests—the Heart Test, the Eye Test, and the Master Test—and each one asks the same question: **Who truly has your heart?**

The Heart Test — What You Treasure Reveal

What You Trust

Jesus begins with treasure because it is one of the clearest mirrors of the soul. Treasure is not merely what you own; it is whatever begins to own your heart. It is whatever rises to the top of your priorities, your desires, your sacrifices, and your decisions.

In the ancient world, treasure was fragile. Moths ate fine garments. Rust corroded tools and coins. Thieves tunneled through soft clay walls and stole valuables. Everything people valued could be lost in a moment.

Jesus is not condemning possessions—He is exposing misplaced security and redirecting our trust.

He redirects our hearts toward a treasure that cannot be touched. Heaven's treasure is not kept in vaults but in lives shaped by obedience, mercy, and a steady trust in God. These treasures are not vulnerable; they are eternal and untouchable.

Jesus reveals a simple truth: *wherever we invest our treasure, our heart begins to follow.* Show me where your treasure is, and I can tell you where your heart lives.

We often think treasure follows the heart—but Jesus reverses it because the heart is more pliable than we realize. The things we consistently invest in—our time, our attention, our resources—slowly shape our hearts to love what we have chosen.

Which raises a question worth asking: **What treasure is shaping your heart right now?**

And the truth is, our treasure doesn't stay silent. It calls to us, it forms us, and it steadily becomes the compass of our lives. What we cherish most eventually shapes what we chase.

The Eye Test — What You Look At Shapes Who You Become

Jesus moves from treasure to vision. In His culture, the eye was understood as the lamp of the body—the instrument that allows light to enter. A "clear" eye was not merely healthy eyesight; it was a Jewish phrase meaning *generous, open-hearted, rightly focused way of seeing*. A "bad" eye referred to stinginess, envy, or a distorted way of seeing reality .

In other words, what fills your vision will quietly shape the direction of your life.

If your eye is generous—fixed on God and attentive to His kingdom —your whole life is filled with light. But if your eye is clouded—by envy, greed, comparison, or fear—darkness spreads.

Which leads to an honest question: **What am I allowing to fill my vision?**

Our lives are shaped by whatever we consistently look at. For some, it's achievement, reputation, financial security, or the approval of people. Jesus warns that a distorted focus doesn't just dim your perspective— it darkens your entire inner life *over time*

Where the heart test searches our desires, the eye test searches our direction. Both shape us—slowly, quietly, and inevitably.

The Master Test — Who You Serve Reveals Who You Love

Jesus closes with the most uncompromising statement in the passage: *"No one can serve two masters."* He does not say it is difficult—He says it is impossible.

In Jesus' world, a servant belonged wholly to one master. Shared ownership wasn't an option. Divided loyalty simply did not exist.

Jesus uses that reality to confront the illusion of spiritual neutrality.

The truth is that every heart serves *something*, and over time what we serve becomes what we love.

Jesus names "mammon" as the rival master—not merely money, but the entire pull of material wealth and possessions that competes for our trust. *Mammon* presents itself as a provider—it offers safety, identity, comfort, status, even control. It whispers that more will finally be enough. But its promises are empty; it can never secure what it claims.

Jesus reveals a simple truth: the human heart **cannot live with divided allegiance**—it was never designed to be shared between God and idols.

This test forces the question: *Who commands my decisions? Who shapes my priorities? Who receives my loyalty when no one else sees?*

The master you obey is the master you love.

The Tests That Free Us

Together, these three tests—treasure, vision, and loyalty—form a single invitation: the invitation to freedom. Jesus is not trying to shame us for caring about earthly things; He is rescuing us from trusting them.

The heart test frees us from false security.
The eye test frees us from distorted focus.
The master test frees us from divided allegiance.

This reflects the spirit of the Beatitudes—a pure heart, a deep hunger for righteousness, and a devotion that is not divided. These tests flow naturally from Jesus' words: *"Blessed are those who hunger and thirst for righteousness."* To hunger for righteousness is to desire a heart aligned with heavenly treasure, a vision illuminated by God's light, and a loyalty shaped by the Father's love.

Jesus is not merely exposing misplaced desires; He is awakening a new appetite within us—the appetite of the kingdom. He is inviting us to re-center our hearts on the King and His kingdom.

Reflection & Practice

Before moving on, take a moment to honestly invite the Holy Spirit to search your heart. These tests are not meant to condemn you but to free you—to reveal what holds you so you can cling more fully to the One who never fails.

- **The Heart Test:** What treasure is shaping your desires right now? What would it look like to store up treasure in heaven this week?

- **The Eye Test:** What has been filling your vision lately—light or darkness? Where is Jesus inviting you to refocus your attention?

- **The Master Test:** What master competes for your loyalty? What step of surrender is Jesus asking you to take so your allegiance is fully His?

Take these tests with you into the quiet places of your week. Let them linger in your prayers and conversations with God. Remember—Jesus gives these tests not to burden you, but to liberate you. As you walk forward, ask Him to form in you a heart that treasures what He treasures, eyes that see as He sees, and a loyalty that rests joyfully in His faithful care.

Chapter 11

The Path of Kingdom First Living

Matthew 6:25-34

25 Therefore, I say to you, take no thought about your life, what you will eat, or what you will drink, nor about your body, what you will put on. Is not life more than food and the body than clothing?

26 Look at the birds of the air, for they do not sow, nor do they reap, nor gather into barns. Yet your heavenly Father feeds them. Are you not much better than they?

27 Who among you by taking thought can add a cubit to his stature?

28 Why take thought about clothing? Consider the lilies of the field, how they grow: They neither work, nor do they spin.

29 Yet I say to you that even Solomon in all his glory was not dressed like one of these.

30 Therefore, if God so clothes the grass of the field, which today is here and tomorrow is thrown into the oven, will He not much more clothe you, O you of little faith?

31 Therefore, take no thought, saying, "What shall we eat?" or "What shall we drink?" or "What shall we wear?"

32 (For the Gentiles seek after all these things.) For your heavenly
Father knows that you have need of all these things.

33 But seek first the kingdom of God and His righteousness, and all
these things shall be given to you.

34 Therefore, take no thought about tomorrow, for tomorrow will
take thought about the things of itself. Sufficient to the day is the
trouble thereof.

Pastor's Reflection

At certain moments in the Sermon on the Mount, Jesus moves beyond instruction and begins to shepherd the heart. Matthew 6:25–34 is one of those moments. His words feel less like a command and more like a rescue—gently but firmly drawing us away from the quiet illusions that keep us anxious.

The longer I sat with these verses, the more I realized how deeply worry runs through the human experience. Not loud, frantic worry, but the quiet kind—the respectable, socially acceptable kind—that whispers about tomorrow and slowly erodes trust in God. Jesus addresses that deeper ache in the soul. He is not shaming His disciples; He is freeing them from the internal captivity of fearing the future.

These words sit at the center of His sermon for a reason. Everything before this moment forms the interior life of a disciple—purity of heart, sincerity of motive, undivided loyalty. But here Jesus turns our eyes outward toward the uncertainty of tomorrow and asks the question every disciple must eventually face: *Will you trust your Father with what you cannot control?*

These verses have stayed with me for many years. It has shaped my prayers and redirected my focus more times than I can count. What astonishes me most is how clearly Jesus ties the promise of God's provision to the pursuit of His Kingdom. Matthew 6:33 was one of the first verses that ever truly gripped my heart: **God Himself promises to meet the needs of those who seek His Kingdom and His righteousness.** That truth echoes back through the Beatitudes—why we must hunger and thirst for righteousness—and forward into the rest of Scripture: "My God will supply all your need according to His riches in glory by Christ Jesus."

I say this often to our church, and I mean it every time: **God**

truly wants what is best for us.

Not what is easiest, not what is most comfortable, but what leads us into the fullness of His Kingdom and the joy of His care. **And His promise is His provision—His faithful commitment to supply what we need as we seek His Kingdom and His righteousness.**

These truths have confronted me, comforted me, and corrected me in profound ways. They have reminded me that worry is not just an emotional habit—it is a spiritual rival. But Jesus, with the gentleness of a Shepherd and the authority of a King, calls us into freedom: a freedom found not in securing tomorrow, but in trusting the Father who already holds it. And every time I return to this passage—especially in seasons of uncertainty—it reminds me again that the Father who cared for yesterday and commands today is already waiting faithfully in tomorrow.

The Burden Jesus Names — When Worry Shapes the Heart

Worry is ancient, but it adapts effortlessly to whatever situation or age we live in. For the first-century Jewish listener, worry centered around daily bread, seasonal harvests, unpredictable weather, and oppressive taxation. For us, it centers around bank accounts, deadlines, diagnoses, decisions, and an endless stream of future hypotheticals. But the result is the same: Worry slowly bends the heart inward until we begin living as though tomorrow depends entirely on us.

Jesus' command, *"Take no thought,"* does not prohibit responsible planning. It confronts **anxious fixation**—the sort of mental rehearsing that turns the future into an idol we must appease. He is not scolding thoughtful preparation; He is calling out fearful fixation.

When Jesus begins with *"Therefore,"* He connects worry directly to what He has just taught about treasure, vision, and loyalty. Worry is not random—it reveals something deeper happening in the heart. When our treasure is misplaced, our vision distorted, and our loyalties divided, anxiety naturally fills the empty space in our hearts. We worry because we fear losing what we treasure most.

And so Jesus turns our attention to necessities—food, drink, clothing—not to shame us, but to expose how quickly good desires can become consuming concerns. Then He invites us outdoors, into a divine classroom beneath the open sky. Birds never sow, reap, or store in barns. Lilies do not spin thread or weave garments. Yet both flourish under the Father's care. Birds display the rhythm of God's daily provision, and lilies reveal the beauty of His intentional care.

If creation—unredeemed, temporary, fleeting—receives such attention, how much more will the Father care for His image-bearers? Jesus is not minimizing our needs; He is reframing them. Life is more than survival, and the body is more than a canvas for worry. We were not created to live crushed beneath imagined tomorrows. We were created to seek the Kingdom today.

The Father Who Is Revealed — When Provision Reshapes Our Perspective

Worry often grows wherever God is misunderstood. Many people imagine God as distant, unpredictable, or emotionally volatile—much like the pagan gods of the ancient world who needed to be appeased through offerings, rituals, and displays of devotion. But Jesus dismantles those assumptions with one phrase repeated throughout this sermon: ***"Your heavenly Father."***

To Jesus' original audience, this was revolutionary. Rabbis occasionally spoke of God as Father in a national sense, but rarely in an intimate, personal way. Yet Jesus uses the term with warmth, frequency, and tenderness. He reveals a Father who is attentive, not abstract; present, not peripheral; generous, not grudging. Worry loses its roots when the Father regains His rightful place in our understanding.

Jesus points our eyes back to creation—not for sentimental comfort, but to show us something true about who God is. Birds and lilies are not merely symbols; they are evidences. Every feeding bird is a testimony of the Father's ongoing involvement in His world. Every blooming flower is a reminder that God's care is not merely functional but beautiful.

When Jesus says, *"O you of little faith,"* He is not rebuking weakness; He is showing where our trust has slipped. Little faith appears when we speak of God with confidence yet picture the future as if He will not be present in it. It is not disbelief—it is divided belief.

Then Jesus contrasts the disciple with the Gentile world: *"The Gentiles seek after all these things."* Their lives were marked by anxious striving because their gods were unreliable. They never knew whether their efforts would secure favor from their gods. Jesus shows the futility of that life and the freedom of Kingdom life. The Father knows what we need. The Father sees what we lack. The Father provides what we cannot.

We do not seek the Kingdom because our needs are small—we seek it because our Father is great And when the Father is rightly seen, worry begins to lose its voice.

The Life Jesus Calls Us To — When Priority Becomes a Pathway

Before looking closely at Jesus' climactic command, it helps to share something personal: **long before this book—and long before this Sermon on the Mount series—the call to "seek first the Kingdom of God" had already begun tugging at my heart.** In 2024, while preaching a series on being *Kingdom Minded*, I was confronted—deeply and unexpectedly—by how easily Christians, myself included, drift into living as if our lives belonged to us. That series planted the seed that would eventually grow into this two-year journey through the Sermon on the Mount.

During that study, Matthew 6:33 resurfaced again and again—not simply as a command, but as a **lens** through which all of discipleship could be seen. I began to notice how much of the Christian life collapses when this verse is neglected, and how much strength returns when it is obeyed. In that 2024 series we asked direct, uncomfortable questions:

Who is really running my life?

What kingdom am I serving?

What am I actually seeking first?

As I sat with those questions, it became clear that Jesus is not calling His people to add the Kingdom to their list of responsibilities; He is calling us to reorder life itself.

Everything in Matthew 6 builds toward the high point of Jesus' command: *"Seek first the kingdom of God and His righteousness."* This is not a slogan—it is the orienting truth of a disciple's life.

Jesus is not rearranging our to-do list but reorienting our desires. Seeking first means the Kingdom becomes the reference point for every decision, every goal, every direction.

To seek the Kingdom is to desire what God desires, to value what He values, and to trust His timing, His provision, and His wisdom above our own. It means we stop building our lives around "What if?" and begin building them around "Your will be done."

It means righteousness is not merely a moral standard but a life aligned with the character of God. This echoes what we explored in that earlier study: **you cannot serve two masters**. The pursuit of righteousness and the pursuit of self-rule cannot coexist. One will eventually bow to the other.

Jesus also exposes the deeper issue beneath material concern—mammon—not simply money, but the mindset that treats material provision as if it holds power of its own. The mindset that says, *"My life, my effort, my outcomes, my control."*

This passage exposes how subtly we begin trusting material provision more than the God who provides. Jesus dismantles that illusion with tender clarity: *"Your heavenly Father knows that you have need of all these things."*

When Jesus promises that *"all these things shall be given to you,"* He is not inviting us into a life of excess but a life of sufficiency. God provides what His children need to fulfill His will. Kingdom-first living is not a call to neglect earthly responsibilities; it is a call to approach them with eternal priorities.

Finally, Jesus brings us back to the burden of tomorrow: *"Do not take thought about tomorrow."* Tomorrow has never answered to our control, and worry has never altered it in our favor. Jesus is not asking us to ignore tomorrow but to stop living as though it rests upon our shoulders. Each day has enough trouble of its own, and the Father meets us in each one with grace for that day.

This is not resignation—it is freedom. It is the life shaped by the Beatitudes: the poor in spirit who trust God's provision, the meek who rest in His strength, the pure in heart who walk with undivided devotion, and the peacemakers who live with confidence in their Father's rule. This is the posture that makes seeking the Kingdom first both possible and joyful.

This passage functions like a hinge in the entire sermon. The Beatitudes prepare us for it. Salt and light express it. Wholeness fulfills it. Undivided loyalty protects it. And Kingdom-first living completes it.

This is Kingdom life—a life freed from anxious striving and anchored in the Father's faithful care.

Reflection & Practice

Before moving on, allow these words to speak into the anxious corners of your heart. Jesus is not calling you to ignore reality—He is calling you to see it rightly. He is not dismissing your needs—He is placing them in the hands of your Father.

- **Where has worry taken root in your life?** What are the deeper fears beneath it?

- **How is the Father inviting you to trust His care in this moment?** Where do the birds and lilies preach a sermon your heart needs to hear?

- **What would it look like—practically—to seek the Kingdom first in this season of your life?** What needs to be rearranged, surrendered, or re-centered?

Bring your tomorrow to the Father—He is already there. And as you walk forward, remember: seeking the Kingdom first is not an obligation but an invitation into a life freed from the tyranny of tomorrow and filled with the presence of God today.

Chapter 12
Handle With Care: The Way We Judge & Restore

Matthew 7:1–6

1 Judge not, that you be not judged.

2 For with what judgment you judge, you will be judged. And with the measure you use, it will be measured again for you.

3 And why do you see the speck that is in your brother's eye, but do not consider the plank that is in your own eye?

4 Or how will you say to your brother, "Let me pull the speck out of your eye," when a log is in your own eye?

5 You hypocrite! First take the plank out of your own eye, and then you will see clearly to take the speck out of your brother's eye.

6 Do not give what is holy to the dogs, nor throw your pearls before swine, lest they trample them under their feet and turn around and attack you.

Pastor's Reflection

There are passages you study, passages you preach, and then there are passages that quietly expose you. Matthew 7:1–6 has been one of those for me. It feels like a mirror—showing more than we expect and inviting us into something harder than we usually want: facing ourselves honestly before we try to evaluate someone else.

Some of the most painful lessons in my ministry have come through strained relationships, misunderstandings, and moments when pride clouded my own vision. More than once, the Lord has gently shown that the real issue was not "out there," but *here*—in my own heart. This passage became a steadying force during seasons of conflict, reminding me that correction cannot come from a heart that has not first been corrected.

One moment still comes to mind. During a tense season in our church—when stress and change were pressing in from every direction—my relationship with a fellow pastor began to unravel. Frustration led to words that should not have been spoken. Assumptions filled in the gaps. Before long, distance had formed between us. When the moment finally came to speak honestly, the Lord revealed that my frustration was rooted less in his actions and more in my own reluctance to obey what God had been calling me to do. The plank Jesus described was not theoretical—it was painfully real. And God used that moment to reshape how I approach people, conflict, and even preaching.

This passage is not calling us to ignore sin or abandon truth. It is calling us to approach people the way Jesus has approached us—with humility, honesty, and genuine love. It is a call to handle people with care because they are image-bearers of God, deeply loved and deeply valuable. And before we ever attempt to help them, Jesus reminds us to let Him help us first.

The Way of Withheld Judgment — A Kingdom Shaped Posture

Jesus' words in Matthew 7:1–6 don't appear suddenly or stand alone. They rise naturally from everything He has already taught. The Beatitudes formed the heart posture of a disciple—poor in spirit, meek, merciful, pure in heart. The call to be salt and light shaped how we influence others. The warnings against anger, lust, and divided motives trained our hearts toward wholeness. The command to seek first the Kingdom aligned our desires.

At this point in the sermon, Jesus turns our attention toward how we treat one another. This is not a new subject—it simply grows out of everything He has already been shaping in the heart of a disciple. A Kingdom-shaped heart will inevitably collide with real people. And it is in those interactions—moments of frustration, hurt, disappointment, or difference—that our true formation is revealed.

Jesus begins with a warning that is less about behavior and more about posture: *"Judge not, that you be not judged."* He is not forbidding discernment. He is forbidding the spirit of superiority that forgets mercy, forgets grace, and forgets the poverty of spirit where this journey began.

When someone truly understands their own spiritual poverty, judgment begins to lose its grip. A person who has mourned their own sin does not find pleasure in exposing someone else's. Meekness refuses to weaponize truth, and a heart that truly hungers for righteousness longs for restoration, not humiliation.

This is why Jesus warns us that the measure we use toward others will be the measure used toward us. It is not a threat—it is spiritual reality. The proud heart becomes increasingly blind. The merciful heart becomes increasingly free.

Seeing Clearly Starts With Seeing Yourself

There is humor in Jesus' picture here—but it is deliberate. The image is almost absurd, because the problem it exposes is painfully real. He is not exaggerating; He is exposing the normal human tendency to see sin in others more quickly than we see it in ourselves.

Seeing clearly begins with letting Jesus adjust our vision. The issue is not eyesight—it is honesty. Before we can understand another person's struggle, we must let the Holy Spirit illuminate our own motives, reactions, and wounds.

A Kingdom disciple must be able to say:

- *My anger may be louder than their mistake.*
- *My assumptions may be louder in my mind than the truth.*
- *My hurt may be shaping my interpretation more than facts are.*
- *My pride may be the real barrier to peace.*

This kind of humility does not appear naturally in us. It grows slowly as we surrender our pride and allow the Spirit to search us. When we pause long enough to let the Spirit search us, we often discover that our conflicts have less to do with others and more to do with what remains unsettled within us

Plank removal is painful—but it is also freeing. When Jesus reveals something in us that needs to be addressed, He does not shame us. He heals us. And once the plank is removed, something beautiful happens: clarity comes. Compassion rises. Defensiveness fades. A desire for restoration begins to form—not to win, not to prove, not to expose—but to love.

Restoring Others With Kingdom Hands

Jesus does not end the conversation by telling us to avoid helping others. He says, *"Then you will see clearly to take the speck out of your brother's eye."* The command is not optional. Restoration is part of discipleship. But only disciples who have been humbled can help others without harming them.

In the Kingdom of God, **correction is never about controlling someone else**. It is about caring for them. When we help someone confront sin, we are stepping into a holy moment. We are touching something delicate. Eyes are fragile. Hearts are fragile. And Jesus invites us to approach them with the same gentleness He has shown us.

A Kingdom disciple restores the way Jesus restores:

- gently, not forcefully
- patiently, not harshly
- humbly, not proudly
- wisely, not impulsively

People are not obstacles to overcome or problems to manage. They are the beloved sons and daughters of God—**pearls of great worth.**

When we offer correction, we are helping remove what is harming them—not merely what is bothering us.

This is why Jesus commands humility before correction. Without humility, truth becomes a weapon. With humility, truth becomes medicine. And when correction flows from love rather than superiority, the goal becomes restoration rather than victory.

Discernment: Knowing When to Speak and When to Wait

Verse 6 may seem disconnected at first, but it actually completes Jesus' teaching about correction. After warning us against hypocrisy, He now warns us against naïve optimism. **Not every heart is ready to receive truth. Not every moment is the right moment. Not every conversation is wise to pursue.**

This is not about labeling people. This is not about labeling people —it is about reading situations with spiritual discernment. Jesus is saying, *"Be wise with what is sacred."*

Some people are still too wounded to hear correction. Some are too defensive for truth to take root. Some are simply not ready for the conversation. Some will attack the messenger because the message feels threatening.

Discernment protects both the one giving correction and the one receiving it. It keeps us from forcing truth where it will not yet bear fruit. It keeps us from pushing a conversation God has not opened. And it keeps us from exhausting ourselves trying to change hearts that only the Spirit can change.

Discernment is love shaped by patience.

Discernment is truth wrapped in wisdom.

Discernment is mercy guided by clarity.

A Kingdom disciple is not silent out of fear—they are measured out of love. They trust the Spirit to open doors, soften hearts, and create readiness.

And sometimes the most faithful thing we can do is wait, pray, and entrust their heart to God's timing.

The Way of Jesus

Every part of this passage ultimately points us back to the character of Christ. He is the fulfillment of everything He is teaching. He never judged with hypocrisy. He never corrected with arrogance. He never spoke without perfect discernment.

Jesus saw our blindness clearly. He knew the weight of our sin and the judgment we deserved. Yet instead of condemning us, He moved toward us with mercy. Yet He approached us with gentleness instead of condemnation. He spoke truth with compassion. He extended mercy before we even knew to ask for it. **Jesus did not merely remove our speck—He bore the plank of our sin at the cost of His own life.**

Because of His sacrifice, we see. Because of His grace, we stand. Because of His Spirit, we can now extend to others what He extended to us.

To walk in the way of Jesus means learning to:

- see others through the lens of mercy
- correct with love rather than pride
- speak truth with patience rather than pressure
- entrust every heart—including our own—to the Father's timing

Jesus does not simply tell us to live this way—**He makes it possible.** And as we walk with Him, the Kingdom way becomes not just something we believe, but something we embody.

Reflection & Practice

Before you speak correction, pause long enough to let Jesus first speak to your heart.

- *What plank might be clouding my view right now?*
- *Am I approaching this person with the humility of the Beatitudes?*
- *Is my desire restoration or vindication?*
- *Do I need to speak—or do I need to wait and pray?*
- *Am I treating this person as a burden, a threat, or a beloved image-bearer of God?*

Correction is sacred work. It requires clean hands, clear eyes, and a humble heart.

Let Jesus steady your vision. Let His mercy shape your tone. Let His wisdom govern your timing.

And may every interaction be marked not by judgment, but by the Kingdom way—**truth wrapped in grace and offered with care.**

Chapter 13

Ask, Seek, Knock: The Open-Hearted Father

Matthew 7:7-12

7 Ask and it will be given to you; seek and you will find; knock and it will be opened to you.

8 For everyone who asks receives, and he who seeks finds, and to him who knocks, it will be opened.

9 What man is there among you who, if his son asks for bread, will give him a stone?

10 Or if he asks for a fish, will he give him a snake?

11 If you then, being evil, know how to give good gifts to your children, how much more will your Father who is in heaven give good things to those who ask Him!

12 Therefore, everything you would like men to do to you, do also to them, for this is the Law and the Prophets.

Pastor's Reflection

Prayer has always stretched my trust—not because God has proven untrustworthy, but because my heart is often slow to believe how willing He really is to care for His children. Matthew 7:7–12 reshaped the way I think about prayer, the way I preach it, and the way I try to shepherd others in it.

In this passage Jesus is not describing a reluctant God or a distant Father. He is revealing a willing Father—One whose posture toward His people is open, generous, and attentive. That vision of God changes prayer far more than any technique ever could. I can trace moments in our ministry where God took these words and brought them to life.

There have been seasons when our church faced real uncertainty—moments when the needs in front of us were larger than our resources and the future felt unclear. During those times we prayed often and waited often. And again and again God answered. Not always immediately. Not always the way we expected. But always faithfully.

Each time He provided, He reminded us of something simple but powerful: the Father's heart is open. He is not irritated by our asking, annoyed by our seeking, or unwilling to answer our knocking. He actually invites His children to come.

Looking back, I can also see how often this passage corrected my own assumptions about God. Where I feared scarcity, He showed generosity. Where doubt crept in, He revealed steady love. Where I hesitated to ask, He kept inviting me to come again.

This passage does more than prepare us to pray—**it shows us the kind of Father Jesus has been pointing us toward all along.** Everything He has taught—loving others, serving others, forgiving others—flows from a life rooted in the goodness of a

Father who gives good things.

Ask, Seek, Knock — The Invitation to Draw Near

Jesus begins this section not with pressure to perform but with an invitation to draw near. The verbs He uses—ask, seek, knock—carry a sense of movement and persistence. They assume relationship. They assume trust.

To ask assumes Someone is listening. To seek assumes Something valuable is available. To knock assumes a Door is ready to be opened.

Jesus is not giving a formula for prayer here. He is revealing the heart of God. Prayer is not about persuading a reluctant God to care; it is about coming to the Father who already does.

And Jesus makes the invitation universal:

"Everyone who asks receives..."

This does not mean God promises to grant every desire we bring to Him. It means the Father will always respond with what is truly good—according to His wisdom, not merely our wishes.

Asking becomes trust. Seeking becomes movement of the heart toward God. Knocking becomes perseverance rooted in confidence.

Through these simple words Jesus is shaping disciples who do not shrink back in hesitation but step forward in faith.

The Father Who Gives Good Gifts

Jesus understands the fear that often sits quietly behind our prayers: *What if God does not answer? What if He remains silent? What if my need is met with disappointment?*

So He gives us a picture we cannot ignore—and it comes with a touch of humor.

A child asks for bread. A father hands him a stone?

Impossible.

A child asks for fish. A father throws a serpent at his feet?

Unthinkable.

Jesus almost invites us to smile at the image. Even imperfect parents know better than this. The dad who burns breakfast, forgets the grocery list, and sends the wrong lunchbox to school still understands the difference between something nourishing and something useless.

And if flawed people know how to give good things to their children, Jesus asks, **"How much more your Father in heaven?"**

Jesus is not portraying God as reluctant or stingy. He is revealing a Father who delights in caring for His children. The Father who does not roll His eyes when you pray. The Father who does not leave you alone to figure everything out.

Jesus is not simply teaching us how to pray—He is teaching us how to trust. *Until we believe the Father is good, prayer will always feel uncertain.*

And the greatest gift God gives is not merely provision itself but His presence revealed through it.

When He gives, He gives wisely. When He delays, He delays with purpose. When He withholds, He does so for reasons we may not yet see.

Every answer we receive is shaped by the goodness of the Father.

When Receiving Becomes Revealing — Grace That Flows Outward

After speaking about prayer, Jesus does something surprising. He shifts the conversation—not to a different subject, but to the natural result of receiving from God. The word "**therefore**" in verse 12 connects everything together. Any time Scripture uses that word, we should pause and ask, *"What is the therefore there for?"* It shows that what comes next grows directly out of what has already been said. It ties the generosity of the Father directly to the generosity of His children.

"Therefore, whatever you want men to do to you, do also to them..."

Jesus is essentially saying: *once you have experienced the generosity of the Father, it will begin to reshape the way you treat other people.*

Too often we treat the Golden Rule as an isolated command—something printed on a classroom poster or quoted as generic morality. But in Jesus' teaching, it is the **fruit** of prayer, the **evidence** of trust, and the **overflow** of grace.

When we ask, seek, and knock—when we receive bread instead of stones, when we receive fish instead of serpents, when we experience the Father's kindness—we are transformed.

When we ask, seek, and knock—and discover that the Father truly provides—our posture toward others begins to change.

- *His* patience softens our impatience.
- *His* mercy quiets our harshness.
- *His* generosity loosens our grip on self-preservation.
- *His* faithfulness steadies our fear.

Grace received becomes grace extended. The kindness we experience from God begins to shape the way we respond to the people around us.

The Golden Rule is not about self-effort. It is about **reflection**. We treat others the way God has treated us. And the more we receive from Him, the more naturally we extend His heart to the people around us.

The Golden Rule — The Kingdom Way in One Sentence

Jesus ends this section with a remarkable statement:

> *"...for this is the Law and the Prophets."*

In other words, the entire direction of Scripture—every command, warning, and invitation—points toward this kind of life.

Do to others what you would want done for you, in light of what God has done for you.

This is not a reduction of God's law but a revelation of its heart. Every instruction God has given ultimately moves toward love shaped by His generosity.

Notice what Jesus does not say.

He does not say, "Do to others what they have done to you."

He does not say, "Do to others what they deserve."

Instead, He calls His followers to treat people the way they themselves long to be treated.

Which raises an important question: *How do we want to be treated?*

With patience when we fail. With mercy when we sin. With compassion when we struggle. With generosity when we are in need. With forgiveness when we repent.

These are the very gifts God has already extended to us.

And so the Golden Rule becomes a Kingdom invitation to embody the Father's heart:

- To move toward people rather than away.
- To assume the best rather than expect the worst.
- To give rather than guard.
- To bless rather than retaliate.

Everything in the Sermon on the Mount has been moving toward this moment—not as scattered teachings, but as a single vision of Kingdom life. The Beatitudes formed our character. Jesus' teachings reshaped our loves, our priorities, and our relationships. Now those inward changes become visible in the way we treat others.

Now, in the Golden Rule, Jesus gathers all of that formation into one sweeping, visible expression: **the Father's heart reflected through His children.** This is where inward formation becomes outward transformation. This is where private prayer becomes public compassion. This is where trust in the Father becomes love for neighbor.

When people are treated with the patience, mercy, and generosity we have received from God, something remarkable happens: they begin to see a glimpse of the Father's heart. In those moments, heaven touches earth.

Reflection & Practice

Prayer is not just a discipline—it is an *invitation* into the *Father's goodness*. Before moving on, pause and reflect on these questions:

- *Am I approaching God as a reluctant giver or a generous Father?*
- *What fears hold me back from asking boldly or seeking persistently?*
- *Where have I seen the Father give "good gifts" in ways I did not expect?*
- *How is the Father's generosity shaping the way I treat others?*
- *Who in my life needs me to extend the same grace God has extended to me?*

Asking leads to receiving. Receiving leads to trust. Trust leads to transformation. Transformation leads to love.

And this is how the Kingdom moves from heaven into our everyday lives—through children who come to their Father with open hands, and then open those same hands to others.

Chapter 14
The Narrow Road: The Choice That Leads to Life

Matthew 7:13-14

13 Enter at the narrow gate, for wide is the gate and broad is the way that leads to destruction, and there are many who are going through it,

14 Because small is the gate and narrow is the way which leads to life, and there are few who find it.

Pastor's Reflection

Matthew 7:13–14 is one of those passages that carries a kind of weight you feel immediately. Jesus does not leave much room for negotiation here. His words press for a decision and force us to face what is truly at stake. They confront us, clarify reality, and refuse to be softened

When I first preached this message, I felt the weight of eternity in a way I rarely had before. I felt it in my study, in my notes, even in the drive to church that morning. The truth is simple: ***Jesus is not describing two opinions or two lifestyles—He is describing two destinies.***

In a culture that prizes endless options and personal customization, Jesus speaks with startling clarity: **in the end there are only two roads**. One leads to life. One leads to destruction. Every person—religious or not—is walking on one of them.

This passage became a kind of mirror in my own life—not because I doubted my salvation, but because it forced me to examine my direction. Am I intentionally walking the narrow way, or am I slowly drifting toward the comfort of the broader road without noticing? The question was not about losing Christ. It was about the posture of my heart toward Him.

And when I looked out at our church—at people I love, at faces I pray for regularly—I realized this passage was not merely instruction. It was an invitation for every heart, whether searching, wandering, or firmly anchored in Christ, to consider the path we are choosing day by day.

The gospel is never a guilt-driven shove. It is a grace-filled call. And Jesus' call here is unmistakably clear: **Enter. Walk. Choose life.**

Some messages strengthen believers. Others comfort the hurting. This one, however, awakens the soul in a way few passages do. It is Jesus, full of truth and full of grace, lifting His voice so the whole world can hear: "There is a road that saves your life—take it."

Two Gates — The Decision Every Person Must Make

Jesus begins not with travel advice but with a command: "*Enter at the narrow gate.*" Before describing the roads or their destinations, He brings us to the place where a choice must be made. A gate is a point of entry—the moment when a traveler chooses one direction instead of another.

There is no middle gate. There is no third path. There is no spiritual bypass that avoids commitment.

The wide gate is easy because it requires nothing—no surrender, no repentance, no faith. It makes no demands because it offers no transformation. Left to ourselves, this is the entrance every human heart naturally chooses.

The narrow gate, however, must be entered intentionally. Not because God delights in making things difficult, but because pride resists surrender. The narrow gate requires humility to admit we cannot save ourselves, courage to turn from sin, and faith to entrust our lives to Christ.

The narrow gate is not a system or a standard—it is Jesus Himself.

He is not one option among many, nor one religion among many spiritual possibilities. He is the only gate because He is the only Savior.

When Jesus says, "Enter," He is inviting us to move from

admiration to faith, from curiosity to surrender, from merely considering Him to truly coming to Him.

Two Roads — The Way of Ease or the Way of Life

After the gates come the roads. Jesus wants us to understand that salvation is not just a moment but a pathway—a lifelong journey shaped by the gate we entered.

The broad road is the road of self-rule. It is crowded because it welcomes anything—any belief, any lifestyle, any pursuit that keeps the self at the center. It sounds appealing: follow your heart, live your truth, define your own path. But what looks like freedom slowly becomes captivity, and its final destination is destruction.

The broad road feels easy, not because it is safe, but because it follows the natural current of the human heart. No repentance is required. No surrender is necessary. Just drift—and you will remain on it.

The narrow road, however, is the road of discipleship. It is narrow not because God enjoys restriction, but because truth has boundaries and love has direction. This path is shaped by the teachings of Jesus, sustained by His Spirit, and marked by obedience that grows over time.

The narrow road may be demanding, but it is deeply good. It leads toward life, toward freedom, and ultimately toward home.

Everyone is on a road, but only one road leads to life.

Two Crowds — Many or Few

Jesus then makes a statement that should slow us down: *many* travel the broad road, but *few* find the narrow one. He is not offering statistics; He is issuing a warning. Popularity is never proof of truth. A crowd does not guarantee safety.

The broad road is crowded because it is comfortable and requires nothing of us. The narrow road is less traveled because it calls for surrender.

Yet there is grace even in this warning: **the narrow road is open to anyone who will enter**. No one is too broken, too sinful, or too far gone to come to Christ. The gate is narrow, but the invitation is wide.

Though few *find* the road, anyone may walk it. Jesus never turns away the one who comes.

The Gospel Call — Enter Through Christ

This passage is not merely an illustration; it is an invitation to respond. Jesus is pleading with the crowd. He does not say, "Study the narrow gate." He says, "Enter it."

Eternal life is not found by admiring Jesus, but by trusting Him.

The narrow gate is not found in:

- church attendance
- morality
- good intentions
- self-improvement
- spiritual curiosity

The narrow gate is a Person.

Jesus is the only way because He is the only One who dealt with what blocked the path—our sin.

At the cross, He opened the way. In His resurrection, He secured the way. By His grace, He invites us into the way.

There are only two paths, but there is one Savior—and His arms are open.

Today—and every day—Jesus offers life: *"Enter... through Me."*

How Do I Enter the Narrow Gate?

Entering the narrow gate is not about repeating certain words or performing a religious ritual. It is the heart turning toward Jesus in honesty, humility, and surrender. Scripture describes this response with beautiful clarity:

1. Admit your need.
"All have sinned and fall short of the glory of God."
We do not enter the gate carrying our goodness—we enter admitting our brokenness.

2. Believe in Jesus.
"Christ died for our sins... was buried... and rose again."
He paid the full price for our sin and opened the way to God.

3. Repent—turn from sin and self-rule.
Repentance is not perfection; it is a change of direction. It is you seeing your sin for what it truly is—deadly, destructive, dishonoring to God—and **hating it enough to turn from it**.
It is putting away the self-rule of your life and allowing Jesus to have rule and reign. It is turning from the broad road not simply because it is dangerous, but because you recognize it leads you away from the One who loves you.

4. Call on Him in faith.
"Everyone who calls on the name of the Lord will be saved."
Those who come to Him are never cast out.

If you desire to enter through Christ, you can respond to Him right where you are. Speak to Him honestly—even simply:

> "Jesus, I know I cannot save myself. I turn from my sin and trust You alone.
> You are the narrow gate—you are the Savior.
> Take my life. I enter through You."

The words are not magic—the faith behind them is what saves.

And the moment a heart turns toward Him, the journey on the road of life begins.

Reflection & Practice

Before you continue reading, slow down long enough to let Jesus' words search your heart:

- *Which gate have I entered—admiration or faith, self-rule or Christ's rule?*
- *Which road am I walking—ease or obedience?*
- *Am I following Jesus, or am I following the crowd?*
- *What step of surrender is Jesus calling me to take today?*
- *Who in my life needs to hear the invitation to the narrow road?*

There are many voices calling you down many roads. Only one leads to life.

The gate is open. The road is ready. The Savior is calling.

Enter—and truly live.

Chapter 15

By Their Fruit: Seeing the Truth Below the Surface

Matthew 7:15-20

15 Beware of false prophets who come to you in sheep's clothing, but inwardly they are ravenous wolves.

16 You will know them by their fruit. Do men gather grapes from thorns, or figs from thistles?

17 Even so, every good tree bears good fruit. But a corrupt tree bears evil fruit.

18 A good tree cannot bear evil fruit, nor can a corrupt tree bear good fruit.

19 Every tree that does not bear good fruit is cut down and thrown into the fire.

20 Therefore, by their fruit you will know them.

Pastor's Reflection

This passage was one of the most unsettling sections of the Sermon on the Mount—not because it is confusing, but because it is piercing. Jesus is not talking about "those people out there"; He is talking about those who appear to belong to God's people. He is talking about voices that sound spiritual, lives that look religious, and ministries that seem fruitful on the surface.

Even before these words were ever shaped into a message, I felt the weight of them settling over my heart. As I studied this passage, a sobering realization settled in: Jesus is warning His church about deception that comes from within. Wolves do not attack from the outside in this passage—they walk in wearing wool.

But the warning did not stay aimed at others for long. It turned inward. This passage forced me to ask a more personal question: what is actually growing in my own life? What fruit is forming in me? Are the roots of my heart deeply anchored in Christ, or are there places where pride, bitterness, or self-reliance are quietly taking hold?

Jesus' words reminded me of something vital: **fruit is not optional for the Christian life—it is inevitable.** The real question is simply this: what kind of fruit is growing?

Then there is the part of the passage most of us instinctively want to skip—the ax at the root. Yet Jesus speaks about it plainly. **The ax does not fall on every tree;** it falls on the trees that refuse to bear good fruit. And He also explains how good fruit is produced—not through effort alone, but through **abiding.** As Jesus later teaches in John 15: "He who abides in Me, and I in him, bears much fruit." A tree produces good fruit only when it remains connected to the source of life.

There is a clear difference between a tree that is alive—drawing life from Christ and gradually bearing the fruit of the Spirit—and a tree whose fruit quietly reveals that its root has never belonged to Him at all.

This truth makes the passage not only instructional but confessional. It reminds us that God does not threaten faithful believers with judgment—He reassures them by contrast. The ax is not poised over the tree planted by the Father, the tree slowly growing in grace, the tree learning to bear good fruit. It is aimed at the tree that refuses transformation, the tree whose roots remain untouched by grace

For the believer, that reality does not produce fear—it produces humility, gratitude, and assurance. And it calls every heart not to anxiety but to honesty. Not to panic, but to repentance. Not to fruit-polishing, but to root-level grace.

Jesus does not expose the root to shame us. He exposes it to save us. The warning is sharp, but the invitation underneath it is full of mercy.

Seeing Beneath the Surface — The Danger Jesus Wants Us to Notice

Jesus begins with a warning that feels abrupt but necessary: *"Beware of false prophets."* These are not outsiders attacking the flock—they are insiders who **appear** to belong. They blend in with convincing language, spiritual vocabulary, even what looks like successful ministry. But Jesus pulls back the appearance and shows us what lies beneath: wolves wearing wool.

What makes this warning so sobering is how easily deception spreads while appearing spiritual. In our time it often travels through social media, influencers, podcasts, and viral clips—voices that speak the name of Jesus while their lives or teaching quietly move people away from Him. Wolves rarely arrive snarling; they arrive convincing. False teaching almost never introduces itself openly. It spreads through half-truths, appealing personalities, and ideas that sound close enough to truth that many people never stop to question them.

Jesus wants His followers to understand that spiritual danger is often subtle rather than loud. It grows patiently. It feels familiar. And at first it may even appear harmless. That is why the real danger is not always in the first words someone says—but in the fruit their life **produces** over time.

False prophets often appeal to our desires more than to God's truth. They promise comfort without repentance, spirituality without surrender, blessing without the cross. The message may soothe the mind for a moment, but it quietly starves the soul.

So Jesus teaches us **where to look**: not at charisma, gifting, personality, or popularity. Not even at short-term results. Those things can hide a diseased root.

Instead, He directs our eyes to the fruit—the long-term evidence of what is truly growing beneath the surface.

This warning is not meant to make believers suspicious of everyone. It is meant to make us discerning. Jesus is teaching His followers to look beyond appearances and pay attention to outcomes. That shift —from surface to substance—is what protects the heart of His disciples.

What Fruit Reveals — How the Heart Shows Itself

Jesus does not leave us guessing. He gives the simplest test imaginable: "You will know them by their fruits." Fruit is the outward expression of an inward spiritual reality. It is the visible revelation of the invisible root.

A healthy root produces good fruit. Not instantly. Not perfectly. But over time, inevitably.

Good fruit begins to appear in humility, repentance, integrity, purity, generosity, faithfulness, and love shaped by the Spirit. Even the Beatitudes describe this kind of fruit: poverty of spirit, mourning over sin, meekness, hunger for righteousness, mercy, purity of heart, peacemaking, and perseverance under pressure.

Bad fruit may look impressive for a time, but eventually arrogance, manipulation, deception, impurity, or self-exaltation begins to surface. The root eventually reveals itself.

Jesus' point is not that we must become spiritual detectives. It is that **truth grows outward**. Over time, the heart shows itself.

And this teaching is not only about others—it is about us as well. Jesus invites His disciples to examine not merely the leaves of our lives but **the root**. Am I abiding in Christ or performing for appearance? Am I living from surrendered dependence or self-sufficient effort? The fruit reveals the answer.

When God Inspects the Root — The Weight of Jesus' Warning

Jesus then brings His listeners to the most sobering part of the teaching: *"Every tree that does not bear good fruit is cut down and thrown into the fire."* Notice what Jesus does **not** say. He does not say that *every tree* will face the ax—only the ones that **do not** bear good fruit.

Jesus is not warning faithful disciples who are growing, stumbling forward, and producing the slow, steady fruit of grace. He is warning those whose lives show no evidence of transformation, whose roots remain untouched by the life of God.

The ax at the root is not aimed at surface behavior—it is aimed at what lies beneath. God does not prune what is spiritually dead—He removes it. He does not polish diseased roots; He replaces them with something living.

This is not meant to terrify the believer—it is meant to awaken the pretender. Jesus is not attacking the struggling Christian; He is exposing the counterfeit faith. He is teaching us that spiritual appearance without spiritual life is a deadly illusion.

But even here, the warning carries mercy. The ax has not yet fallen—there is still time. The time of inspection is coming, but not yet come. There is space for repentance, for honesty, for the gospel to do its deep work underground where no one else can see.

The root Jesus seeks is not perfection. It is transformation.

Reflection & Practice

The words of Jesus in this passage are meant to slow us down—not to create fear, but to foster discernment, honesty, and deeper abiding. Before rushing past this warning, allow His imagery to read *you* as much as you read it.

Consider prayerfully:

- **What does the fruit of my life consistently reveal about the root of my heart?** Not the polished parts—the consistent parts.

- **Where do I see the life of Christ already producing good fruit in me?** Even small growth is real growth.

- **Where am I tempted to focus on appearance instead of abiding?** Where am I managing leaves instead of tending roots?

- **Are there any attitudes, habits, or hidden places where unhealthy roots have begun to grow?** What is Jesus gently bringing into the light?

And as you reflect, remember this: **Jesus never warns without offering Himself as the remedy.** The call is not to self-improvement but to abiding.

Let His warning draw you into His presence. Let His grace make you whole.

When the root is surrendered to Christ, the fruit will inevitably follow.

Chapter 16
When Good Works Become a False Savior

Matthew 7:21-23

21 Not everyone who says to Me, "Lord, Lord," shall enter the kingdom of heaven, but he who does the will of My Father who is in heaven.

22 Many will say to Me on that day, "Lord, Lord, have we not prophesied in Your name, cast out demons in Your name, and done many wonderful works in Your name?"

23 But then I will declare to them, "I never knew you. Depart from Me, you who practice evil."

Pastor's Reflection

Some passages in Scripture have a way of exposing things we would rather overlook. This is one of them. These are not the words of a prophet thundering judgment or an apostle correcting error—these are the words of Jesus Himself. And they are aimed not at the openly rebellious, but at the person who assumes they are already safe.

This passage presses an uncomfortable question into the open: **Is it possible to be busy with spiritual things and still lack real spiritual life?**

Before these verses were ever formed into a message, I felt the weight of them settle in my heart. They pressed on me a truth I could not escape: **good works can become a false savior.** They can camouflage a root untouched by grace. They can create confidence where there should be trembling. They can produce noise without relationship.

And yet, even in this sobering warning, there is mercy. Jesus does not say, "I once knew you, but you drifted too far." He says, **"I never knew you."** The issue is not failure—it is absence of relationship. Not stumbling—it is never having surrendered to Him in the first place.

This passage is not written to frighten the believer, but to wake up the self-confident. It exposes the difference between performing for God and actually being known by Him—between good works used to build an identity and good works that flow from one.

And beneath all of it is this mercy-laced truth—Jesus is willing to know us. He is willing to receive, redeem, forgive, and transform.

But He will not be an accessory to our self-salvation projects.

My hope in this chapter is simple: that it slows us down long enough to be honest. Not to stir fear, but to bring the kind of clarity that leads us back to the only Savior who can truly save.

This warning also turns my heart toward gratitude rather than fear. Before Christ saved me, I was doing what so many in this passage did—leaning on my own good works, believing they made me right with God. I was active, sincere, and convinced that my efforts meant something. But at twenty years old, the Lord opened my eyes to the truth that my goodness could never save me. What I needed was not more effort, but His grace. These words from Jesus, far from driving me into despair, make me lift my hands in worship. They remind me of the mercy that rescued me, the grace that found me, and the Savior who knows me.

When Saying "Lord, Lord" Isn't Enough — Exposing False Assurance

Jesus begins with a phrase that feels jarring precisely because of who He applies it to: *"Not everyone who says to Me, 'Lord, Lord,' shall enter the kingdom of heaven."* These are not casual observers. These are not people indifferent to God. They are people emotionally engaged, verbally expressive, spiritually active—and still spiritually lost.

In the ancient world, repeating a name—"Lord, Lord"—was a sign of deep emotion, urgency, or affection. These individuals are not cold toward Jesus; they are passionate. Yet passion without surrender is still rebellion.

Jesus is showing us that saying the right words does not mean the heart is truly surrendered.

A person can know the vocabulary of faith, say all the right things, sincerely believe they are devoted, and still never have bowed their heart in repentance and trust. It is possible to speak about Jesus fluently without ever submitting to Jesus fully. Familiarity with spiritual language can create the illusion of intimacy, and religious expression can quietly replace genuine dependence. Jesus is exposing a heart that wants the benefits of faith without the surrender faith requires—a heart that confesses Him with words while resisting Him with the will.

This is not Jesus critiquing weak believers. He is exposing hearts that want the language of discipleship without the life of discipleship. Hearts that want Jesus as a concept, not as King—a reality later seen even in the life of His own disciple Judas Iscariot.

The problem is not that they spoke about Jesus—it is that they never truly yielded to Him.

When Ministry Becomes a Substitute for Surrender — The Danger of Empty Religion

"Have we not…?"

Their defense reveals their deception.

"Have we not prophesied in Your name… cast out demons… done many wonderful works?"

These are not average accomplishments. These are the kinds of things we would celebrate in any church. These individuals had impressive résumés. They had ministry success. They had credentials that many would envy.

But Jesus is not measuring activity. He is looking deeper—at the root of the life behind it.

This is where the danger of empty religion becomes clear: **good works can deceive us into thinking we are good.** Ministry can become a mask that hides an unchanged heart—serving replacing surrender rather than flowing from it.

They list what they *did* for Jesus, but never mention what Jesus *did* in them. They can recount their works, but they cannot point to His transforming grace.

And this is the sobering reality: **a person can do many things that look like kingdom work and still not belong to the King.**

Activity is not assurance. Accomplishment is not salvation. Spiritual gifting is not spiritual rebirth.

Jesus is not moved by what we have done for Him—He is moved by whether we belong to Him.

"I Never Knew You" — The Tragedy of an Untransformed Life

Few words in Scripture land with more weight than these: *"I never knew you. Depart from Me."*

Not, "You didn't do enough." Not, "You tried but failed." Not, "You used to follow Me, but you drifted."

Jesus says something far more devastating and revealing: **"There was never a relationship to begin with."**

This is not the anguish of the believer who sinned. It is not the lament of the Christian who stumbled. It is not the confession of someone who wrestles and repents and clings to Christ.

These words are directed at people who were close to the things of Jesus—but never truly united to Him.

To those who were around the things of God—but never surrendered to the Son of God.

To those who wanted the benefits of the kingdom—but never bowed to the King.

"I never knew you" means:

- You performed for Me, but you never came to Me.
- You worked for My approval, but never received My grace.
- You wanted My power, but not My presence.
- You loved ministry, but not Me.

It is not that Jesus refuses relationship—it is that **they refused it**. They chose doing over knowing. Earned identity over received grace. Religion over redemption.

This passage becomes a mirror for every disciple: *do we actually want Jesus,* or *only what we hope He will do for us?*

The Hope Behind the Warning — A Relationship That Saves

If this chapter ended with "Depart from Me," we would be undone. But warnings in Scripture always carry mercy, and Jesus' words also reveal the path of life.

First, Jesus says: *"He who does the will of My Father."* This is not perfection—it is direction, marked by repentance, obedience, and ongoing transformation. It is a life shaped by repentance, surrender, and ongoing transformation.

Second, the entire Sermon on the Mount has shown us what doing the Father's will looks like. Throughout Jesus' teaching we've seen the shape of a transformed life: poverty of spirit, mourning over sin, meekness, hunger for righteousness, mercy, purity, peacemaking, trust in the Father's care, seeking the Kingdom above all else, and bearing good fruit. These are not works we perform to earn salvation—they are the evidence of salvation at work within us.

The hope of the gospel is not that we manage to prove ourselves to Jesus, but that He **receives** and **transforms** those who come to Him by faith.

He does not say, "Try harder and I will accept you."

He says, "Come to Me, and I will make you new."

The warning is serious, but the invitation of grace remains open.

Gospel Invitation — The Savior Who Knows You

If this passage has unsettled your heart, that is mercy—not condemnation. The Spirit disrupts false assurance so that true assurance can take its place.

Here is the good news: **Jesus saves all who come to Him in repentance and faith.** Not by works. Not by spiritual achievement. Not by religious performance.

Repentance means turning from sin and turning away from self-salvation. It is letting go of the illusion that your goodness can save you. It is hating your sin enough to walk away from it and surrendering the rule of your life to Jesus.

Faith means trusting in Him alone—His work, His cross, His resurrection. It is receiving, not achieving. Resting, not performing.

If you sense the Spirit calling you, you can respond with a simple, sincere prayer—not a formula, but a cry of surrender:

"Jesus, I come to You with nothing but my need. I turn from my sin and from trusting in myself. I believe You died for me, rose for me, and offer forgiveness and new life. I surrender to You as Lord. Know

me, save me, make me Yours."

When someone comes to Jesus this way, He does not turn them away.

He does not weigh résumés. He does not measure spiritual output. He receives the sinner who comes in truth and grants what religion can never produce—relationship.

To be known by Jesus is not to be perfect; it is to be His. It is to live no longer striving to prove yourself, but resting in the grace that has already claimed you. Those whom Christ knows, He keeps. Those whom He saves, He transforms.

And this is the promise the gospel holds out: everyone who comes to Him will be forgiven, received, and known by Christ—not for a moment, but forever.

Reflection & Practice

Before you rush past this passage, allow its sobering clarity to lead you into honest reflection:

- **Am I trusting in Christ alone, or am I secretly leaning on my works?**
- **Is my relationship with Jesus personal or merely performative?**
- **Do I obey because I love Him—or because I want to be seen as spiritual?**
- **Where is Jesus calling me to surrender rather than strive?**
- **What evidences of grace—however small—confirm the work of the Spirit in me?**

This is not a call to fear but a call to clarity—not to doubt God's faithfulness, but to examine our own hearts.

Let the warning drive you to Jesus—and let His grace assure you that those who come to Him in truth are never turned away.

Remember this: Jesus does not expose false assurance to condemn you—He exposes it to rescue you. His words are an invitation to step out of empty religion and into a living relationship defined by trust, surrender, and love.

Take time this week to sit with Him in prayer. Ask Him to search your heart. Invite Him to deepen your dependence on His grace. Rest in this promise: those known by Christ are kept by Christ.

Chapter 17
The Blueprint for a Life That Endures

Matthew 7:24-27

24 Whoever hears these sayings of Mine and does them, I will liken him to a wise man who built his house on a rock.

25 And the rain descended, the floods came, and the winds blew and beat on that house. And it did not fall, for it was founded on the rock.

26 And every one who hears these sayings of Mine and does not do them will be likened to a foolish man who built his house on the sand.

27 And the rain descended, the floods came, and the winds blew and beat on that house. And it fell. And its fall was great.

Pastor's Reflection

In 2023, the Lord began opening my eyes to something foundational—something I hadn't fully recognized in all my years of ministry. I saw that while many churches, including ours, had labored faithfully to evangelize, we had not always been equally faithful in **discipling** *people after they came to Christ.*

One Sunday I asked our church a simple question: "How many of you had someone personally walk with you after salvation and teach you how to build your life on a solid foundation?" Only a few hands went up. That moment stayed with me. It humbled me and made me realize something needed to change.

I began praying, "Lord, help us rebuild from the ground up. Help us become a church that doesn't just lead people to Christ but teaches them how to follow Him."

That prayer reshaped everything.

We devoted 2024 to the commands of Christ—because Jesus Himself said in the Great Commission, "Teach them to observe all things whatsoever I have commanded you." These commands are not suggestions; they are the **foundation stones** of a life built on Him.

And then the Lord kept bringing me back to the Sermon on the Mount. As I worked through it slowly and prayerfully, something began to come into focus. **If the commands of Christ are the foundation, then the Beatitudes and the rest of the sermon show us what a life built on that foundation actually looks like.**

A house is built to be seen. And our lives are meant to visibly reflect the character, values, mercy, purity, and priorities of Christ. Everything Jesus preached in this sermon was not theoretical—it was how He lived. And now He invites us to build the same kind of life, on the same kind of foundation.

So when Jesus ends the sermon with the story of two builders, He isn't switching topics. He is bringing everything together. **Every life is building something, and sooner or later every foundation is tested.**

This final teaching of Jesus is not meant to frighten us but to free us. It calls us back to the simplicity and power of hearing and obeying. It reminds us that storms do not destroy what is built on Christ—they reveal it.

The Wise Builder — Hearing and Doing

Jesus begins with the person who hears His words *and does them.* This is more than intellectual agreement or emotional response. It is active trust. It is alignment of life with His teaching. It is obedience shaped by faith and fueled by surrender.

The wise builder understands something simple but important: **storms will come, but they do not have to destroy a life built on the right foundation.**

Obedience becomes the anchor, surrender shapes the structure, and Christ Himself is the rock beneath it all.

This builder digs deep—not because it is easy, but because it is necessary. Building on rock requires effort, intention, and perseverance. It means reordering life around Kingdom priorities, reevaluating desires, repenting often, forgiving freely, seeking righteousness, and trusting the Father's heart.

In other words, it means everything Jesus has already described in the Sermon on the Mount.

Obedience is not a single moment; it becomes the pattern of a life that is being changed by Christ.

And Jesus says of such a life: *"It did not fall."*

Not because the house was strong, but because the **foundation** was.

The Foolish Builder — Hearing Without Responding

Then comes the contrast—not between believer and unbeliever, but between hearing and obeying.

Both listen. Both understand. Both build.

But only one obeys.

The foolish builder makes a quiet but serious mistake—**he assumes that hearing Jesus is enough.** He treats agreement or admiration as if they were the same thing as obedience.

But Jesus makes it unmistakably clear—

A house built on knowledge without obedience will not stand.

Sand is easier. Faster. More convenient. It allows a person to build without changing, construct without surrendering, appear religious without being transformed.

And for a time, it works. Until it doesn't.

For a while the foolish builder's house looks just as strong as the other one. But when the storm comes, the weakness of the foundation is exposed.

The issue is not the house, but the heart. Not the craftsmanship, but the foundation.

Disobedience is not a small crack—it is a structural failure waiting to happen.

The Storm That Tests Every Life

Jesus chooses words that are intentionally universal: *"the rain descended, the floods came, the winds blew and beat on that house."* He is describing more than weather—He is describing the human experience. Every life, no matter how carefully constructed or outwardly stable, will eventually face pressures that reveal what lies beneath the surface.

Storms show up in many ways—pressure, suffering, temptation, unexpected loss, deep disappointment, and ultimately the day we stand before God.

These realities do not single out certain kinds of people; they touch every life without discrimination. Storms do not reveal who we hoped to be—they reveal who we truly are: what foundation we trusted, what truth we embraced, and what strength we depended on.

For the wise builder, storms become evidence of a deeper stability. They reveal that the foundation is solid, that obedience was not wasted effort, and that Christ truly is enough to hold a life together.

But for the foolish builder, the storm reveals what was always there: a foundation that could not hold the weight of real life.

Jesus is not warning us merely about the existence of storms; He is preparing us to face them with confidence. And His message is unmistakable: **you will not outlast the storm unless your life is anchored to the Rock.**

The Collapse — When the Foundation Fails

Jesus does not soften His words: *"And great was its fall."* The collapse He describes is not a minor setback or a temporary crack—it is total, devastating ruin. The house may have looked strong, its frame may have appeared impressive, and its builder may have felt confident, but when the foundation failed, everything built upon it fell with undeniable force.

That collapse is the outcome of building a life on something other than Christ.

Self-reliance eventually buckles under the weight of reality. Cultural Christianity cannot withstand spiritual testing. Religious activity without surrender cannot hold a heart together.

Selective obedience may seem stable for a time, but when pressure comes it cannot hold.

Yet Jesus' words are not spoken to shame but to save. The warning carries an invitation—an opportunity to rebuild before the storm arrives.

The wise builder is not the one who never struggled, never stumbled, or never questioned. The wise builder is the one who returns again and again to the true foundation.

And the promise Jesus gives still stands—**those who build their lives on the Rock will stand.**

Reflection & Practice

As you consider Jesus' closing picture, allow His words to steady and search you. The wise and foolish builders are not two different kinds of *knowledge*—they are two different kinds of *responses*. The difference is obedience. The difference is surrender. The difference is foundation.

Reflect prayerfully on these questions:

- **Where am I building quickly instead of building deeply—** and what would it look like, in this season, to "dig deep" into the Rock through rhythms and habits that strengthen my life in Christ?

- **How have past storms revealed the strength—or weakness—of my foundation?** What did they teach me about where my trust truly lies?

- **Is there an area where I admire Jesus' words but resist obeying them?** What step of obedience is He inviting me to take next?

- **Where am I relying on my own strength instead of anchoring myself in Him?** What needs to shift for Christ to be the true foundation?

Remember: The wise builder is not the one who builds perfectly, but the one who keeps returning to the Rock. Storms will come. Winds will blow. Pressure will rise. But the life anchored to Christ will stand—not because strength is ours, but because the foundation is unshakable.

Chapter 18
The King and His Kingdom

Matthew 7:28-29

***28** When Jesus finished these sayings, the people were astonished at His teaching,*
***29** for He taught them as one having authority, and not as the scribes.*

Pastor's Reflection

Sometimes Scripture pulls the curtain back and people suddenly realize they are seeing things clearly for the first time. That is what happens at the end of the Sermon on the Mount. Matthew says the crowds were astonished. They knew they were hearing something very different from the teaching they were used to.

They weren't listening to another rabbi explaining the Scriptures. They were listening to Someone who spoke with the authority of the One who gave them.

For the past two years, as our church has slowly walked through these chapters, something similar has happened in my own heart. The more I studied Jesus' words, the more I felt their weight—not just the wisdom in them, but the authority behind them. Little by little it became clear that the sermon is not only teaching us how to live; it is revealing who Jesus truly is.

And in this final moment, everything comes into focus. It reveals who has been speaking the whole time.

After immersing myself in the Sermon on the Mount for so long, I realized something profound: the sermon is not great because the teaching is unmatched—it is great because the Teacher is unrivaled. Every word flows from the King Himself. The One who calls us to this Kingdom is the One who reigns over it.

That realization also changed how I looked at the opening chapters of Matthew. The Sermon on the Mount shows us what life in the Kingdom looks like, but Matthew 1–2 introduces us to the King Himself—His arrival, His identity, and His mission.

His beginning, His Beatitudes, and His blessed hope all point to one truth: **the King has come, and His Kingdom is advancing.**

Ending this book by looking at Jesus' authority simply makes sense. The Sermon on the Mount is not just a collection of moral teachings—it is the voice of the King calling His people to live under His reign.

The Authority of the King

Before Matthew records a single miracle—before Jesus casts out a demon, stills a storm, or multiplies bread—the people already recognize something unmistakable: His authority does not come from earth.

The scribes taught by quoting other scholars. Jesus taught by speaking truth as the standard Himself. His authority was inherent, not borrowed. When He said, *"You have heard it said... but I say to you,"* He wasn't offering commentary—He was issuing commands.

The Sermon on the Mount shows us that authority in several ways.

1. Authority Over Interpretation

Jesus does not explain the Law—He fulfills it. He reveals its truest meaning. He speaks with the clarity of the One who wrote it. And He restores the Law's original intention: not as a tool of oppression, as the Pharisees had twisted it to become, but as a gracious beacon pointing people to their need for a Savior and to the heart of the God who gave it.

2. Authority Over Humanity

Every command in the sermon calls for wholehearted allegiance. Jesus speaks not only to outward behavior but to the inner life—motives, desires, and the orientation of the heart. No earthly teacher can make such demands, but Jesus can, because He alone has the rightful authority to rule the human heart.

3. Authority Over Destiny

Jesus also speaks clearly about the judgment to come. His warnings are not guesses or opinions. Only the Judge of all the earth can speak this way.

This is why the crowd is astonished. They see, perhaps for the first time, what the Sermon on the Mount has been telling us all along: **the One on the mountain is no mere teacher. He is the King.**

The Kingdom Has Come

The final words of Matthew 7 draw our eyes upward. But to understand the weight of Jesus' authority, we must look backward —to the opening chapters of Matthew.

Before a sermon was preached, before a disciple was called, before a miracle was performed, the King arrived—not in a palace, but in a manger. *Heaven announced it plainly: a Savior, Christ the Lord, had been born.*

When Jesus arrives, the Kingdom arrives with Him.

Angels announced it. Shepherds witnessed it. Magi traveled across a great distance to see it for themselves.

This King was not elected, appointed, or inherited through human lineage—He was born King.

The Kingdom began not with human achievement but with divine initiative. In a quiet village, under Bethlehem's sky, the King stepped into His world to reclaim His people and establish His rule.

When Jesus climbed the mountain to preach, He was not launching a philosophy—He was declaring the values, priorities, and identity of His Kingdom.

The Character of the Kingdom

If the King has come, then what kind of Kingdom does He bring? The Sermon on the Mount answers this question with every verse.

This Kingdom is not political, military, or cultural in the way people expect. It is a Kingdom that changes hearts.

It is a **transformational** Kingdom.

The Beatitudes describe its citizens—humble, merciful, pure, peacemaking, hungry for righteousness. These traits are not natural; they are supernatural. They are the evidence of a heart reshaped under the rule of the King.

The commands describe its ethic—one that refuses hatred, rejects lust, reconciles quickly, loves enemies, gives secretly, prays sincerely, forgives freely, seeks the Kingdom first, and builds on the Rock.

This Kingdom does not advance by force but by transformation. Its borders expand every time a heart bows to the King, every time a believer obeys His voice, every time His people reflect His character in a world shaped by pride and power.

The Mission of the Kingdom

The Sermon on the Mount is not merely a description of Kingdom life—it is a call to Kingdom mission.

Jesus came not only to transform His people but also to send them.

This mission appears clearly in the sermon:

- *"You are the salt of the earth."*
- *"You are the light of the world."*

- *"Let your light so shine before men."*

The mission is clear: **make the King known by living out His Kingdom.**

This mission is continued in Jesus' later words: *"Go and make disciples of all nations..."* The sermon forms the content; the Great Commission forms the command.

We are sent into the world as representatives of the King— not to seize power, not to secure influence, not to preserve comfort,

—but to display His character and proclaim His reign.

The world sees the Kingdom every time it sees His people obey the King.

The Kingdom in the Present

The Kingdom is not only something that *has come* and something that *will come*—it is something that **is here now**, advancing quietly but powerfully through the lives of those who belong to the King.

Jesus described this present reality when He taught His disciples to pray, *"Your Kingdom come, Your will be done, on earth as it is in heaven."* This is not wishful thinking; it is a daily invitation.

Every act of obedience, every moment of mercy, every step of forgiveness, and every choice to pursue righteousness are ways the Kingdom quietly shows up in this world.

This present Kingdom does not arrive with spectacle but with transformation. It takes root in ordinary places—homes where grace begins to win, workplaces where integrity begins to matter, communities where reconciliation replaces resentment, and churches where real discipleship begins to flourish.

The Kingdom is present wherever the King's people embody the King's ways.

And though its advance is often quiet, it is never weak. Jesus declared that the gates of hell will not prevail against His Church—not because the Church is strong, but because the King is present.

The Sermon on the Mount is not merely an ideal to admire but a reality to live. It is the King's blueprint for what the world should see **right now** through His people.

The Future of the Kingdom

The Sermon on the Mount ends with astonishment, but the story of the Kingdom does not end there. The King who spoke with authority will one day return with power.

The future of the Kingdom is not uncertain. God has already promised it.

The prophets saw it. Jesus proclaimed it. The apostles lived for it.

One day, the meek will inherit the earth—not metaphorically, but literally. One day, righteousness will not be hungered for—it will fill the world. One day, peacemakers will not just be blessed—they will reign with the Prince of Peace.

Revelation gives us the final picture: *"The kingdoms of this world have become the kingdom of our Lord and of His Christ, and He shall reign forever and ever."*

The sermon points us to that day. The King's authority at the end of Matthew 7 is a preview of His authority over all creation. The question is no longer simply, *"Will His Kingdom come?"* but *"Am I living for it now?"*

Reflection & Practice

As you conclude this journey through the Sermon on the Mount, let Jesus' final scene shape your heart. The crowds were astonished because they recognized something undeniable—the King had spoken. His authority was not partial, borrowed, or negotiated. It was absolute.

Let these questions guide your reflection:

- **Where have I admired Jesus' words without submitting to His authority?**

- **What part of my life still resists living under the reign of the King?**

- **How is Jesus inviting me to reflect the character of His Kingdom in this season?**

- **Where is He sending me to live out the mission of the Kingdom?**

- **How does the future hope of the Kingdom reshape the way I live today?**

The King has come. His Kingdom is advancing. And one day, His reign will be fully seen and fully felt.

Until that day, may our lives be built on His words, shaped by His character, directed by His mission, and anchored in His unshakable authority.

Pastor's Final Reflection

For the past two years, our church family has stood together at the feet of Jesus on the mountain, listening as He spoke words that have reshaped hearts for more than two thousand years. Writing this book has not simply been a preaching project or an academic exercise—it has been a deeply personal journey of being formed, humbled, corrected, comforted, and called higher by the voice of the King.

When I first stepped into this study, I believed the Sermon on the Mount would make me a better preacher. Instead, it made me a different person.

These chapters exposed my motives, refined my desires, and slowly taught me to treasure the quiet work of God more than the applause of people. I felt the Spirit pressing these truths into my life in early mornings, in long nights of prayer, in hallway conversations, and in ordinary moments that suddenly felt sacred.

My prayer is that as you read these pages, you sensed the same invitation I have sensed again and again—the invitation not merely to study Jesus' teaching, but to follow Him as a true disciple. *The invitation to live the Mountain Life in the ordinary places of everyday life.*

You have not just read a book; in a sense, you have climbed the mountain with us. You have listened to the heartbeat of the Kingdom. And now, as you step away from these pages and back into the world, my prayer is that the words of Jesus continue to echo in you—guiding you, steadying you, and shaping you into the person He is forming you to be as you join the journey of *Becoming the People of the Mountain.*

A Call to Live the Mountain Life

As you step away from these pages and back into the rhythms of your daily life, I urge you not to leave the mountain behind. The Sermon on the Mount was never meant to be admired from a distance; it was meant to be lived.

Jesus did not call us merely to study His words, but to live them. To forgive freely. To love sacrificially. To walk humbly. To trust deeply. To shine brightly.

This journey has reminded me again and again that the Mountain path is not the easy way—but it is the way of life, the way of freedom, and the way of Christ Himself. My prayer is that you will continue growing, stretching, and surrendering as you learn what it means to become more fully each day, *one of the People of the Mountain.*

A Final Blessing

May the Lord who first spoke these words on a hillside speak them anew to your heart. May His Spirit strengthen you to walk the narrow path with courage, joy, and steady hope. May His presence meet you in every valley, and may His voice lead you upward into the life He is calling you to live.

And may you—right where you are, in your home, your work, your community—become one of those people shaped by the Mountain, living proof of the grace and goodness of the Kingdom.

May His peace guard you. May His love empower you. May His Kingdom come in you, and through you, until the day we see Him face to face.

Amen.

If you would like to listen to the full sermon series that shaped this book, you can find it on our church's YouTube channel or on Apple Podcasts and Spotify by searching for *Victory Fallon*. My prayer is that these teachings continue to strengthen your walk with Christ as you grow in the way of the Mountain.

With love and gratitude in Christ,

Appendix A: The Sermon On the Plain

The primary biblical text for the Sermon on the Plain is found in Luke 6:17–26.

The Gospel of Luke gives us a parallel teaching of Jesus often called *The Sermon on the Plain*. While it shares several themes with the Sermon on the Mount, it is clearly a distinct moment in Jesus' ministry—addressing disciples in the presence of the watching crowd.—spoken at a different time, in a different setting, and with a unique pastoral focus.

This appendix is designed to help you see how Luke's account complements the mountain sermon we have studied so deeply. It offers us another angle, another tone, and another invitation into Kingdom living.

1. The Setting of the Sermon on the Plain

In Matthew, Jesus delivers His sermon on a mountain to His newly called disciples—an intimate setting focused on forming their identity. In Luke, the scene unfolds differently. After an all-night prayer meeting and the formal calling of the Twelve, Jesus comes *down* from the mountain to a level place where a different, much larger and more diverse crowd has gathered—disciples, the curious, the hurting, and the skeptical.

Where Matthew emphasizes the private formation of disciples, Luke shows us Jesus ministering among the people before turning His attention specifically to His followers.

Both sermons reveal the heart of Jesus, but their settings hint at different purposes:

- **The Mountain**: Formation, identity, the inner life of the Kingdom.
- **The Plain**: Application, confrontation, the outward realities of living in the Kingdom amid a watching world.

2. The Plain Beatitudes: Personal, Present, and Physical

Luke's Beatitudes press the Kingdom into lived experience—making blessing personal, present, and tangible. It is shorter—four instead of eight—and far more direct. Instead of saying *"Blessed are those..."*, Jesus says, *"Blessed are you..."*

This immediately tells us something: Jesus is speaking intimately and individually to His disciples.

A. A Personal Message

The Sermon on the Mount describes the character of Kingdom people. The Sermon on the Plain applies those truths personally. Jesus looks directly at His disciples and names their present condition—poor, hungry, grieving, rejected—and speaks blessing into it.

This reminds us that the Kingdom is not merely a set of principles; it is a personal relationship with a King who sees us, knows us, and speaks to us individually.

B. A Present Message

Luke emphasizes the *now*: hungry *now*, weeping *now*, hated *now*. Jesus is not only concerned with eternity—He acknowledges the present struggles His followers face.

The Kingdom of God is both **already** and **not yet**. Jesus comforts His disciples with the promise that their present circumstances are not the final word.

C. A Physical Message

Luke does not replace spiritual emphasis with physical concern—he reveals how deeply the two are intertwined in the Kingdom of God.

Where Matthew focuses strongly on spiritual realities, Luke highlights physical, earthly conditions. Jesus speaks into hunger, poverty, grief, and persecution with compassion and hope.

This does not diminish the spiritual message—it enriches it. Our King is not distant. He is moved by our weaknesses and understands our needs.

Those who follow Jesus discover that everything they need is ultimately found in Him.

3. The Pointed Woes: A Kingdom Reversal

A striking difference between the two sermons is Luke's inclusion of four *woes*. Where Matthew gives blessings, Luke provides warnings to those who are self-sufficient, comfortable, and craving the approval of the world.

These woes are not condemnations of wealth, joy, or good reputation—but of misplaced trust.

- **Woe to the rich**: Those who treat earthly comfort as ultimate.
- **Woe to the full**: Those who feel no hunger for God.
- **Woe to those laughing now**: Those who mask emptiness with entertainment.

- **Woe to those praised by all**: Those who compromise truth for acceptance.

Together, the Beatitudes and the Woes function as a mirror—revealing whether our lives are anchored in the Kingdom of God or in the comforts of the present world.

The world exalts independence, indulgence, and image. Jesus exalts humility, dependence, and faithfulness.

This is the great Kingdom reversal.

4. The Message for Us Today

The Sermon on the Plain complements the Sermon on the Mount by calling us to examine the hidden allegiances of our hearts.

Where do we look for joy? For security? For affirmation? For purpose?

Are we trying to find our blessedness outside the Kingdom—constantly leaving the "makarios island"—the place of deep, God-given blessedness to chase what cannot satisfy?

The Sermon on the Plain calls us back. Back to Jesus. Back to dependence. Back to a joy greater than circumstance, a hope deeper than the present moment, and a Kingdom stronger than this world's shifting values.

Reflection & Practice

As you consider Luke's Sermon on the Plain alongside Matthew's Sermon on the Mount, take a moment to reflect on how these teachings intersect with your life right now. Jesus spoke to real people in real circumstances—hungry, grieving, misunderstood, longing for hope. He speaks to us in the same way today.

Reflect

- Where do you presently feel poor, hungry, or weary—and how might Jesus be speaking blessing into those places?
- Are there areas where you've been looking for satisfaction or identity outside the Kingdom?
- Which of Jesus' warnings feels most pointed for your heart? Why?
- How does seeing both sermons together broaden your understanding of what it means to follow Jesus?

Practice

- **Name your now.** Take time this week to honestly identify your present struggles or needs—physical, emotional, or spiritual—and invite God into them.
- **Stay on the makarios island.** Instead of running to other places for comfort or meaning, consciously choose to seek God first in moments of stress or longing.

- **Reevaluate your treasures.** Examine where your resources, energy, and desires are being directed. Ask the Spirit to realign them with the Kingdom.

- **Choose Kingdom joy.** Whether you are in a season of laughter or of weeping, intentionally root your joy in Christ rather than circumstance.

May these reflections and practices guide you deeper into the life Jesus invites His disciples to live—on the mountain, on the plain, and in every ordinary moment between.

Appendix B: The Christmas Prayer

The following devotional reflections are drawn from the Christmas series inspired by the Lord's Prayer and serve as a companion to the themes explored throughout this book. Each movement invites us to see how the coming of Christ reveals the heart of prayer.

1. Our Father in Heaven — The God Who Welcomes Us In

Matthew 6:9a
"Our Father who is in heaven..."

The first words Jesus taught us to pray are words of relationship, not ritual. Before He taught us to ask, to seek, or to surrender, He taught us to approach. Christmas is the story of a Father who opened the way for His children to come home. As we see in the coming of Christ, access to the Father was not earned by goodness—it was granted by grace.

Through Jesus, the distant becomes near. The holy becomes accessible. The Almighty becomes Abba. The manger is proof that God has drawn close, not because we deserved Him, but because He desired us.

Reflection:
Where do you need to remember that God is not distant from you today? How does the coming of Christ reshape your view of God as Father?

Practice:
Approach God in prayer this week as a child—honest, open, unhurried. Let your heart remember that you are welcomed in.

2. Hallowed Be Your Name — The Glory We Long For

Matthew 6:9b
"Hallowed be Your name."

Christmas reminds us that the holy God made Himself known—not in thunder or smoke, but in a child wrapped in cloth. The God whose name is above every name stepped into our world that His name might be honored in our hearts. When we pray, "Hallowed be Your name," we are not merely announcing God's holiness—we are inviting our lives to reflect it.

The angels declared His glory. The shepherds hurried to see it. The wise men bowed before it. And still today, the glory of God shines in the face of Jesus Christ.

Reflection:
Where is God inviting you to honor His name more fully? What parts of your life need to reflect His holiness more clearly?

Practice:
Set aside a moment each day this week to worship God for who He is. Speak His names, recall His attributes, and let awe rise within you.

3. Your Kingdom Come — The Hope That Will Not Disappoint

Matthew 6:10a
"Your kingdom come..."

Christmas is the arrival of the King and the breaking dawn of His Kingdom. The manger is not just the beginning of a story—it is the invasion of light into darkness, hope into despair, and life into a world marked by death. When we pray, "Your kingdom come," we are praying for the reign of Jesus to rule first in us.

The Kingdom came with Christ. The Kingdom continues through His people. And one day, the Kingdom will come in fullness when the King returns. Until then, our hope is not pinned on changing circumstances, but on an unchanging Christ.

Reflection:
Where is the Holy Spirit inviting you to surrender more deeply to the reign of Christ? What area of your life needs Kingdom transformation?

Practice:
Choose one tangible way to embody Kingdom living this week—an act of mercy, forgiveness, generosity, or witness.

4. Your Will Be Done — The Joy of Surrender

Matthew 6:10b
"Your will be done on earth as it is in heaven."

Jesus came in full surrender to the Father's will. Christmas is heaven's "Yes" breaking into earth's "No." The joy of Christmas is not merely that Christ came—but that He came willingly, gladly fulfilling the Father's plan of redemption.

Surrender is not losing—it is trusting. It is believing that God's will is better than our own, that His ways lead to joy, and that His plans are always rooted in His goodness. When we pray, "Your will be done," we are not resigning—we are rejoicing.

Reflection:
What area of your life is hardest to surrender to God's will? What holds you back from trusting His goodness?

Practice:
Pray a simple prayer of surrender each morning this week: *"Father, I trust Your will today. Lead me, guide me, and help me to say yes."*

5. Amen — The Final Word of Christmas

Matthew 6:11–13
"For Yours is the kingdom and the power and the glory forever. Amen."

Every prayer has a final word. For the believer, "Amen" is not just an ending—it is an agreement, a declaration that God is worthy of trust. The Amen of Christmas is the confidence that the God who came still comes, still saves, still leads, and still reigns.

To say "Amen" is to rest in His provision (daily bread), to embrace His forgiveness (debts forgiven), to walk in His victory (deliverance from evil), and to worship His glory. Christmas is God's great Amen to His promises—and our invitation to echo it with our lives.

Reflection:
Where do you need to say a fresh "Amen" to God? Where do you need to trust Him again, rest again, or worship again?

Practice:
End each day this week by praying, "Amen. So be it, Lord." Let that word quiet your fears and strengthen your faith.

ABOUT THE AUTHOR

Aaron McBride is a *husband, father,* and *teacher of God's Word* whose greatest joy is helping people see the beauty of Jesus and the power of His Kingdom. His journey began in Georgia, where God stirred a calling in his heart long before he fully understood where that calling would lead. In 2021, that call brought him and his family across the country to Fallon, Nevada, to serve a local church that had been without a shepherd for two years. What began as an act of obedience quickly became a story of God's faithfulness, renewal, and grace.

The years that followed were marked by transformation—not only within the church, but within Aaron himself. Before the two-year journey through the Sermon on the Mount began, he spent countless Sundays teaching through various books of the Bible and leading a year-long study in *the commands of Christ.* When that journey through the Sermon on the Mount finally began, something deeper took root. What started as another verse-by-verse study became a personal reshaping of his heart, his prayer life, and his understanding of what it means to follow Jesus.

These years left an imprint that would ultimately form this book: **Becoming the People of the Mountain**.

Aaron has had the privilege of witnessing God work in remarkable ways—*lives changed, families restored, hearts awakened to the gospel.* Along the way, God has opened doors for meaningful ministry within the Fallon community, providing opportunities for outreach, evangelism, and spiritual renewal that continue to shape the life of the church.

Yet beyond the moments of public ministry, Aaron's greatest joy is found at home. He and his wife, **Renee**, are grateful to share life, love, and ministry with their five children—**Aric, Alex, Alton, Ariel, and Ashley**—who bring laughter, purpose, and depth to every season of their journey.

Aaron writes with the conviction that he is not a special man, but a servant of a gracious God. His passion is simple: *to help people see the beauty of Jesus, to hear His voice in Scripture, and to live the kind of life Jesus describes on the mountain*—a life shaped not by religion, but by relationship.

Becoming the People of the Mountain is offered with that hope in mind: that readers would not only understand the words of Jesus, but be transformed by them. That they would discover, as he did, that *the way of the Kingdom is not distant or unreachable, but near, present, and available to all who will follow the King.*

Aaron continues to serve, teach, and walk with the people of Victory Church in Fallon, trusting that the same God who called him into the desert is the God who still moves mountains—and shapes the people who stand upon them.

www.ingramcontent.com/pod-product-compliance
Lightning Source LLC
LaVergne TN
LVHW040223110826
845146LV00004B/1261
9798999702012